A white lady who waits at a bus stop by the ruins
of a nunnery, but vanishes when the bus stops.
A coach is drawn through Bradgate Park by four
black, headless horses. Factories on Frog Island that
have been exorcised. 'Ordinary' houses with
inexplicable sounds of chains rattling and doors
slamming. A multitude of pubs and rectories with
supernatural 'residents'.

Leicestershire has a wealth of tales of ghosts,
hauntings, poltergeists and other anomalous events.
In *Ghosts and hauntings in and around
Leicestershire* the experienced paranormal
researcher Andrew James Wright recounts
these reports and attempts to understand
what is really going on.

Andrew James Wright was born in Leicester in
1955. His previous publications include *The Ghosts
of Braunstone Hall, The Lively Ghosts of
Leicestershire* and *Haunted Leicester.* An active
ghost researcher for 30 years, these days he prefers
lecturing about the subject.

Ghosts and hauntings
in and around
Leicestershire

Andrew James Wright

Heart of Albion

Ghosts and hauntings in and around Leicestershire

Andrew James Wright

Cover photograph of Grace Dieu Priory by Bob Trubshaw

ISBN 1 872883 99 0
EAN 978 1872 883 991

Published by
Heart of Albion Press
62 Wartnaby Street
Market Harborough LE16 9BE

albion@indigogroup.co.uk

Visit our Web site: www.hoap.co.uk

Printed in England by Booksprint

Contents

Preface

Leicestershire has a healthy population of haunted locations. In the mid-1970s researcher Andrew York read through back issues of local papers and identified eighty places in Leicestershire and Rutland with ghostly associations and another fifty or so in Leicester itself. Many of these accounts were brief and often quite similar.

Since then many more sightings and anomalous experiences have been reported.

In some instances I have examined the cases personally and have put forward several theories. Ghosts seem to remain tantalisingly anonymous when searching them out – maybe a flash of blue light or a shadow caught in peripheral vision or a quick blast of chill air is all one may find. They appear seemingly at random and when it suits them.

The two counties have phantoms of historical figures, nuns, airmen, lords and ladies, Romans, murderous wretches, hitchhikers and even a steam train. They appear in cinemas, schools, shops, museums, pubs, factories, hotels, in fact just about anywhere!

I began investigating in 1976 and have examined several hundred cases. A short chapter on the rudiments of ghost hunting is for those who may wish to search out these elusive phantoms.

I have peeled away at much of the embellishment these stories gather over the years and present them in good faith as authentic, well-documented true ghost encounters in a variety of haunted places.

Andrew James Wright

July 2006
Leicestershire

Acknowledgements

My grateful thanks to Alison Fearn, Dorian and Kim Gamble, Amanda Gardner, Norman and Maureen Green, Brian Johnson, Michelle Jones, Samantha Lambpet, Susan McLean, Bill Melia, Nevin Moledina, Tom Smith, Norman Waugh, Val Weafer, Tony Webster, and Andrew York.

Sources

History of Bradgate, Marie Forsyth, 1974

Haunted Harborough (VHS Video), Mike Eason, Eason & Roberts Productions 1998

History and Antiquities of Leicester, John Nichols, 1804

Tarona's Ghostly Encounters, Gail Hawkins, Echo Press 2000

The History of the Mysterious Papillon Hall, Colonel Pen Lloyd, Lutyens 1977

The Folklore of Leicestershire and Rutland, Roy Palmer, Sycamore Press 1985

The Ghosts of Grace Dieu, Joanne Brown and John Dickinson, Pukka 2004

The Lively Ghosts of Leicestershire, Andrew James Wright, published by author 1998

The Vale of Belvoir, Michael Honeybone, Barracuda 1987

Brooksby Hall

Brooksby Agricultural College lies just off the busy A607 near to the small village of Brooksby. The building has long held the reputation for being haunted by a ghost called 'The White Lady.'

The origin of the ghost seems unclear but is assumed to be connected with a female skeleton discovered on the site in 1892. Builders knocked a wall out in order to install two large water tanks and found the gruesome scene. There was also a skeleton of a small child. The remains were later placed in a timber chest. A grave was dug by the local blacksmith, then the vicar conducted a short service. Later the bones were buried; unusually this funeral was carried out after dark.

The ghost was usually seen around the staircase and the main hall. In the late 1940s, the owner, Earl Beatty, allowed part of the hall to be used by servicemen convalescing after hospital treatment. There is no record of any soldiers encountering the ghost but one of the volunteers who would visit the hall to help cheer up the men did.

Mrs Barnsley who lived at nearby Hoby was a regular visitor and often stayed overnight. She not only saw the whitish figure on the staircase but also heard, then outside observed, a grand coach pulled by four horses. After the initial experiences Mrs Barnsley adopted the sensible attitude of not being afraid and accepted the visions that she saw many times after as the interesting and mind-provoking events they indeed were.

Today the ghosts seem to have faded with time and there have been no recent reported sightings. On rare occasions though, residential students may complain of being not alone, as if being watched.

Bosworth Hall

Bosworth Hall has a long and complicated history. The first recorded inhabitants were the de Stoke family who had a long period of tenure from 1293 until 1537. A Mr Erasmus Smith, the Lord of the Manor of Bosworth, resided there until 1616, making many significant changes to the building. One of his young sons was thought to be possessed by the Devil! Apparently he would terrify people with his impressions of animals such as cats, dogs and even horses. Such was the superstitious attitude at the time, witchcraft was assumed to be the cause. This eventually led to the somewhat extreme measures of rounding up a total of nine local women and having them hanged as witches.

The 'witches' had been brought in to exorcise the child, whose fits and violent behaviour were more likely to be the result of a mental condition rather than demonic possession. Their failure to 'remove' the evil forces must have led to the notion that the witches were on the side of the Devil and therefore must be dealt with accordingly. They were tried for being implicated in the bewitching of the son of Erasmus Smith. They were all put to death at Leicester Gaol on 18 July 1616.

Shortly after this drama Erasmus Smith himself died, a sorry end to a morbid business. Bosworth Hall was then purchased by Lady Grace Fortescue. She lived there with her son William. The Fortescues were staunch Catholics who had to keep their faith secret to avoid the severe penalties dished out. On one occasion word got through that a raiding party of soldiers were in the vicinity. The priest, who was in the chapel room, panicked in his haste to remove all evidence and make his escape, knocking over a chalice containing the consecrated wine. Apparently this left a dark red stain that remains visible to this day. He made his escape by a secret panel that took him upstairs to a priest hide cleverly built into the wall itself.

Priest hides and holes were a common feature in houses great and small. I have seen a few in my time. One ancient manor house, Chingle Hall in Lancashire, has a somewhat cunning if rather dangerous priest hide. Just about large enough to secrete a small person is an alcove built into the main chimney some eight feet up from the hearth. One would hope the troops would come during the summer months otherwise the hapless priest would be burned or smoked to death!

In 1763, Francis Turville, the cousin of Maria Alethea Fortescue, inherited Bosworth Hall. Later Frances added the Turville to his name. His son, George Fortescue, built onto the house adding a drawing room, and in 1873 his son, Frances, built a church in the grounds. Eight years later Frances married the widow of Baron Lisgar Adelaide who was twenty-four years his senior.

She refused to change here name, even when Frances was knighted. Lady Lisgar made many improvements to the house and outlived her husband by twenty-one years, dying in 1902.

There is a story of Lady Lisgar haunting Bosworth Hall. A staunch Protestant, she is said to have refused entry to a Catholic priest who was summoned to the hall to perform the last rites to a dying servant. Lingering from feelings of guilt, the mournful shade is glimpsed from time to time wandering the winding corridors and stairways. A doctor visiting the house passed her in close proximity on a stairwell. She totally ignored his polite greeting; he only realised it was a ghost when he looked back in disdain to see her vanish.

In 1907 the hall was taken by Oswald Petre, Frances's cousin. After his death in 1941 his widow, Margaret, continued to reside here.

Parts of the hall were let to a number of various families during the Second World War and several detachments of the American forces were billeted inside the building and bivouacs outside in the grounds.

After the war, the house was inherited by the daughter, Alethea, and her husband, David Constable Maxwell. By now the hall was somewhat the worse for wear. Much work was carried out and in 1976 the couple moved into an apartment at the top of the house. Later, their eldest son, Robert, and his wife, Susan, took the house. Robert, a keen landscape gardener planted a vast number of trees and created several spinneys, naming them after past occupants. Today, Bosworth Hall is a plush country hotel.

As well as the shade of the formidable Lady Lisgar there may be another phantom abroad. There is a tale of the young daughter of one of the incumbents who came to a watery end. The girl, Jane, took a liking to the dashing son of one of the gardeners. Slowly, their relationship blossomed. What with the strict social levels of the time their meetings remained clandestine. However, her father got an inclination and banned her from seeing the young man. Of course they paid little heed and over a period of several weeks the father began to follow his daughter to observe their secret meetings. They met at a regular time quite near to a wooden bridge which the young man crossed over and left by.

The father determined he would teach him a lesson. One night he got a stout tree saw and went out to the bridge and fiendishly set about weakening the structure. Later that night, as usual, the pair left their rooms to meet up. One this occasion, for some reason, the young man was late leaving and Jane wondered what had become of him. Concerned, Jane went to see where he was. She was halfway across the bridge when it collapsed and she was drowned.

3

A mournful presence is reputed to linger in her old room just above the main entrance hall.

Another version is that in the sixteenth century, Anna, daughter of the master of the house was having an affair with a yeoman. Her enraged father left a large animal trap out to ensnare the young man. Unfortunately it was Anna who was caught in the rusty iron jaws and who then fainted with shock and lay bleeding heavily. She was discovered next day and taken up to her room. She had lost a lot of blood and sadly died nine days later. It is said that to this day there is an indelible mark of a large bloodstain on the floorboards of her old room. Apparently it also seeped through the ceiling above the large fireplace in the main hall. The stain can no longer be seen as the floor has now been carpeted.

The more likely idea for the bloodstain concerns the priest mentioned earlier. The Roundheads did enter the hall but found no evidence of Catholicism and left. The priest, in his haste, had apparently cut himself quite badly while rushing to his hide. Later when all seemed safe, the family went to tell the priest it was safe to emerge. They were shocked to find the priest dead in the hide; he was partly sodden with communion wine and much blood. The blood and wine soaked through and stained the floorboards to this day.

Casting a critical eye on the matter may suggest that the ghost or ghosts here might have had their origins embellished and distorted. Certainly the indelible stain does exist and many attempts have failed to eradicate it. As to whether it is blood or red wine remains unresolved.

There are quite recent reports of rapid fluctuations in temperature in several of the rooms. It is a fact that for many years the old drawing room retained a constant chill that even the balmiest summer could not penetrate.

The most recent reported sighting occurred in the late 1990s. A flight engineer had to vacate the hotel at the ungodly hour of 3 a.m.. He left his room then opened the fire door that led to a small staircase down to the reception area. To his surprise there was a lady standing at the foot of the stairs. There had been a wedding reception held earlier and the flight engineer assumed she was a bridesmaid as her dress was of a very rich white material. The man gestured to her to ascend the narrow stairs. She seemed to pay him no attention then simply turned and faded away.

Ghosts at work

Ghostly presences inhabit all manner of places, not just bleak ruins, churchyards and ancient manor houses. You may encounter one whilst at work. In 1970 when I worked at F.W. Woolworth & Co Ltd (as it was then known) on Gallowtree Gate in Leicester I was told of the ghost. Apparently it was only seen once late at night by the night-watchman – his dog went mad as a result! How much truth was in it I cannot say but the huge cellars could be a little unsettling if alone down there.

I have it on good authority that two other shops on Gallowtree Gate have a ghost: the sites presently occupied by Ann Summers and Marks and Spencer. As to who the supposed ghosts are remains a mystery.

* * * *

One of life's pleasures is a trip to Melton Mowbray on market day, Tuesdays. The cattle market with its auctions from anything from a small tractor to a ferret, the flea market, the heaving pubs and rustic atmosphere and, I might add, sausages. Some Belgravians and those further afield will remember Sid Atkins, the butcher on Melton Road, Leicester. The best sausages known to man! His son took over the business and apparently altered the recipe, the end of an era. Ken Woodcock, a schoolmaster, sadly no longer with us, went on a mission, to find a decent sausage. He travelled far and wide, often to Spalding in Lincolnshire; with boundless enthusiasm he would bring us half a pound and await the verdict. 'They weren't bad Ken, but... '. Then he found Derek Jones' little shop in Melton Mowbray and the search was over. Apparently a ghost resides with this busy meat purveyor. It has not been seen but heard, although not in recent years. Mr Jones has little time for such ideas but some years ago one of his staff stayed late to prepare some meat. Whilst in the back prep-room he was surprised to hear a series of footsteps moving about the room above. An intruder must have got in. With trepidation, the man slowly went upstairs and searched but found no one at all, puzzled, the man went back to his task.

The next morning he mentioned the mystery to Mr Jones who scoffed at him. Some days later Mr Jones mentioned the phantom intruder to the owner of the premises, Mr Sharpe, who agreed and took it with a pinch of salt. When Mr Sharpe next met his brother he in turn mentioned the supposed ghost and was taken aback at the response.

He recalled their aunt speaking of the ghost in the old cottage, now the butcher's shop. Mrs Saxton had resided there in the 1930s. Intrigued, Mr Sharpe lost no time in contacting her. She explained that indeed it was haunted by an unseen force. She had heard it moving about the place on numerous occasions. The ghost has been dormant for many years. The sausages are the best in England but should the recipe ever be changed I hope the ghost will rattle its chains with vigorous fury!

* * * *

Factories are also places where ghosts turn up. I remember in the early 1980s, an ex-employee of the vast British Shoe Corporation warehouse on Scudamore Road, Braunstone Frith, telling me of a ghost said to haunt the place. He had not seen it himself but several people had. It was unlikely to lead to an investigation as the firm tended to 'play down' the alleged phantom.

Apparently the ghost would just appear from nowhere. It was a man running frantically as if in panic. He had blue-grey serge clothing like wartime RAF personnel. The spectacle would last for just seconds then diminish. Sometimes an appearance would be accompanied by the smell of burning and in some cases just the burning smell with no appearance. There was also unexplained shouting and moving cold spots that would come and go. There was no pattern and the occurrences were spontaneous.

A similar apparition had been reported in two other factories in the vicinity. In one case it was of a man screaming mutely with what looked like flames licking from him.

The theory to account for the haunting is that the site was once an airfield, Leicester Municipal Aerodrome. It was used as a training facility during the Second World War. In 1942 there was a tragic accident when a plane coming in to land crashed into one of the buildings resulting in the death of the pilot. Towards the end of the war there were rumours of a ghost haunting the airfield. And, of course, a place-centred apparition created by a rapid death would be still in his own time dimension. For him it is still 1942 and he is totally oblivious as to what stands there now or those who witness his desperate pleas.

* * * *

Two factories in close proximity in the Frog Island area of Leicester were the scene of inexplicable happenings and both cases were quite unique. Britella Hosiery on New Pingle Street had endured such a high level of supernatural disturbance that the workers were driven to take drastic action. Terrible sensations of an evil presence, persons being prodded by unseen fingers, a blackish mist and other unpleasant events were having an understandably detrimental effect and upsetting some of the women. Complaints were made to the management but no one took the reports seriously. In 1970 several women decided to go to the top with their concerns. If nothing was done the women would walkout and if need be, strike!

The management were dumbstruck; they would have to take these claims a bit more seriously. What did one do? Who deals with this kind of thing? Enquires were made and a clergyman, an archdeacon from Loughborough, was brought in. He performed a service of deliverance, a mild form of exorcism. There was indeed a change afterwards with just minor incidents that eventually ceased altogether.

* * * *

A belt and brace manufacturer situated on Frog Island itself attracted the attention of an unwelcome ghost for a few weeks in early 1992. Icy chills and an invisible presence unnerving some of the workforce become a quite a regular occurrence. Then someone was horrified to witness a grinning old woman wearing a bright pink dress who vanished in a flash.

The mysterious phantom was hampering production and affecting the staff so a psychic medium was consulted. She spent almost an entire Sunday in the building hoping to calm things down or help the confused spirit on its way but failed to make contact.

Meanwhile, the landlady of the pub next door, the North Bridge Tavern, had noticed the absence of their lively pub ghost, 'The Pink Lady'. After several weeks the ghost was sensed and seen back in the pub. The landlady thinks the ghost was merely curious as the factory had stood empty for some time before the belt company took it.

* * * *

Many will remember the old cattle market in Leicester. It covered a vast area of land now called Freeman's Park, a bland, nondescript area with a supermarket, car park, cinema, car showroom and two pubs. The only reminder we have of the popular market are the old original gates.

The huge slaughterhouse had a mysterious ghost by the name of 'The Weasel'. He was rarely seen but certainly heard and performed quite amazing feats. Probably his best performance was re-penning a large number of pigs overnight. Historian Brian Johnson who furnished the account wonders if his presence is still felt around the site.

* * * *

A sock factory in Carey's Close, Leicester had a succession of strange events including a waste bin that moved several feet, icy blasts and most oddly one office was opened early one morning and every surface had a fine dew on it! Several appearances of a man suggestive of the 1930s, a factory worker, were reported. These events lasted for a few weeks then ceased. The building is presently empty.

* * * *

The old Walkers Crisps factory at Thurmaston called in a paranormal investigator after several sightings of a mysterious dark figure were reported in 1982. After a quite exhaustive evaluation the clairvoyant revealed the findings.

The figure was apparently an RAF pilot or flight crew. He was dressed in a bulky flying suit with a zippered front and a fur collar. He had a severe short 'back and sides' and was quite young, around his mid-20s. The hypothesis for the haunting was that the airman was very attached to his plane; this is quite common with aviators. His plane had crashed in 1942. The clairvoyant researched the area and established that a scrap metal yard existed on the site. She 'felt' that his wrecked plane was brought there where it remained for quite a few years. The airman was in trauma and earthbound. After the long attendance by the investigator there were no further reported sightings.

Other ghosts connected to factories include the unmistakable image of Mr W.A. Atkinson who was said to appear at the now derelict Atkinson Hosiery on the end of Canal Street in South Wigston.

A hooded monk has for a good number of years scared employees at the Old Donisthorpe fabric dyers on Bath Street in Leicester. The firm have now moved so the listed building remains empty but the old monk will still be wandering.

Shady apparitions also inhabited the Pool Lorrimer and Taberer hosiery factory on King Street and Frears Bakery on Abbey Lane, Leicester.

Office workers are by no means exempt from a visit by mournful spirits and mischievous poltergeists. There was the time honoured tradition of haunting phenomena in the form of icy chills, eerie sensations and bumps and bangs over quite a long period at a building on Archdeacon Lane near Belgrave Road, Leicester. The old Department of Health and Social Security offices were, for much of the time, busy – well chaotic really. Occasionally during rare moments of quiet there would be a change in the atmosphere, a slow build-up of a morbid feeling, a depressive-ness that on two occasions preceded an appearance of a man wearing a long white coat.

No one had any idea who he was or why he was haunting the place. As is often the case curiosity got the better of one of the workers, so she investigated. She found no record of any dastardly deed, suicide or tragedy that might have caused a restless soul to linger. However her eventual theory was that the mysterious visitor might have been a man by the name of Higgins.

Mr Higgins worked for the travel pioneer, Thomas Cook at his offices on Gallowtree Gate and became a friend of the family, particularly Annie Elizabeth, one of the daughters. In 1880 they became more than friends and marriage was on the horizon. Unfortunately tragedy struck, Annie Elizabeth died either by drowning in the bathtub because the family was against the marriage or by inhaling carbon monoxide fumes from a faulty water geyser whilst lying in the bath at the family home in Stoneygate.

The site of the DHSS offices used to be the Archdeacon Lane Baptist Church where Thomas Cook was a deacon. Annie Elizabeth was leader of the Young Women's Bible Class. After the tragedy, Thomas Cook had a marble bust of his daughter sculpted and placed in the church, also a large leather-bound album containing many letters of sympathy and condolence. In the latter 1930s the church closed.

The theory is that the grief-stricken Higgins visited the church and treated the bust and papers as a shrine to his beloved. Even after death his mournful frustration and anger remained stuck here slowly building up to its oppressive zenith then retiring again.

* * * *

A familiar landmark in Market Harborough is Welland House in the main square. It has been the home of the Market Harborough Building Society since 1961. One day in 1992, Julie was sitting at her desk

Welland House. A mysterious phantom typist is said to linger here.

when suddenly the electric typewriter began clicking away vigorously all by itself. She stared in disbelief at the machine as the keys rapidly depressed then abruptly ceased. Julie looked around at her colleagues, was it some sort of office joke? No one appeared to be paying much attention or stifling giggles. Puzzled, Julie stared back at the typewriter, well aware something was going on.

She told her friend Tracy about it later who then told her of a possible ghost. Apparently shortly after the society took offices in the building the caretaker heard a typewriter clicking away one evening. All the staff had gone, she was sure of that. She went upstairs to the second floor; the typing was coming from the manager's office. The caretaker knocked and entered, the clicking ceased instantly. The typewriter which sat on the secretary's desk was silent and covered.

Julie had thought to retain the message typed and tried to make sense of it:

> The head and in frontal on an English
> writer that the character of this point is
> therefore another method that the time of
> whoever told the problem for the
> unexpected.

It made no sense at all. Was there a memory facility on the machine? If there was, the long sentence was certainly not something one would type up in connection with banking culture. Had it been a joke it would have been humorous or something she could fathom. Intrigued, Julie decided to find out. She noted the make and model of the machine then telephoned the office supply company. She was informed that that particular model had no memory function. A bizarre mystery if ever there was.

* * * * *

An early morning window cleaner had a fright in Cank Street, Leicester. He was halfway through 'blading' a shop front when he noticed a figure inside watching him. He just appeared. It was not a dummy or he would have noticed it earlier. The figure, a man, was very tall and dressed quite oddly; he had a wide brimmed hat and a very long coat with boots that appeared to have something like spurs attached. The window cleaner was so unsettled he ran into a casino across the road.

The Curzon, Loughborough

A cinema in Loughborough, the Curzon, may have a wraith mournfully drifting about the dark corridors and auditoria. Not far away, on the corner of Woodgate and South Street, there used to be a little greengrocers shop run by Isabella Newell. Her husband, John, had spent much of his life in the Royal Marines based at Plymouth then later came to Loughborough as a recruiting officer. After he was pensioned off, he used some of the proceeds to purchase the shop where they also lived.

Unfortunately their marriage was less than blissful. John became increasingly reliant on alcohol and sometimes would become quite violent. He was convinced Isabella was having an affair with a cattle drover who lived nearby on Southfield Road. On the night of 20 August 1894 a terrible row broke out and during a fit of drunken rage, John savagely struck Isabella several times with an iron coal pick. He was later tried for murder and was hanged in the market place before nearly 4,000 braying rabble.

For many years various members of the cinema staff have experienced unexplained cool draughts and the feeling of a presence about the place. Eileen, an usherette for over 30 years, is convinced the place is haunted.

On the night of 31 October 2001, twenty members of staff were locked in the building overnight in order to raise funds for the Variety Club of Great Britain. Loughborough-based ghost-hunter Paula Christodoulou became involved and arranged to attend the event as adviser and she invited me along also. Hallowe'en in a haunted cinema!

I came over early in the evening with work colleague, Phil Rimmer, in his fancy red Toyota MR3 – a very speedy journey from Leicester University to Loughborough! I had to rope in a few 'ghostbusters' for a live TV broadcast on the local six o'clock news, including Darryl Wood. Paula was there and had brought her teenage daughter, Katerina, along – little did she know she would not be going 'trick or treating' later on but a tour of some of the local spooky areas before going home.

After the TV interview I returned to the town centre to locate a decent pub where I could get a hearty meal. I wound up in a raucous Wetherspoons alehouse surrounded by drunken students, some were dressed as ghosts and vampires, but the meal was edible. I then wandered the town until I found a quiet pub until 11 p.m. – peace and quiet at last!

On my return to the cinema I met the staff and Barry Phillips again, Barry was the manager, we had met briefly earlier on during the TV chaos. Paula was already busy setting her laptop computer to test sound filters with Extremely Low Frequency (ELF) experiments, (ELF is sound between 1 and 30 Hz, and totally inaudible). Throughout the night, Paula would ask questions on a digital recorder then allow for an answer that would not be heard at the time, this would then be enhanced to see if a 'response' from a discarnate entity was evident. Other apparatus consisted of an ultraviolet light unit, image intensifier, electrostatic fields monitor, two radios, an infrared video camera, 35mm still camera, a torch with a red filter on the beam and a thermocouple.

Barry had made certain our night would be a comfortable one and had laid on a large selection of sandwiches and sundry snacks plus fresh tea and coffee on tap to help to battle the fatigue that would inevitably set in.

A 'sneak preview' of supernatural thriller, *The Others* was to be shown in one of the small auditoriums so we all gathered and got comfortable. Too comfortable for some as I nodded off and snored throughout the last hour of the film. Then it was time to do some work, let the sport commence!

Paula took a radio and headed off to the large snooker and leisure suite. I was content to sit in the large foyer chatting to the staff and answering their questions on ghosts. One young lady spoke of one auditorium in particular where she and a few others felt ill at ease if alone. Several of the staff were already in there so we went in. A dark, quiet cinema auditorium is an eerie place indeed and the acoustics can play tricks. The general feeling of the staff was that the ghost is no problem whatsoever and quite a few would very much like to see Isabella, if that is who the ghost may be. It all seemed quiet as we sat spread out in the darkness. I later sat alone in the same auditorium but nothing unusual occurred.

While coffee was served in the foyer, Paula returned from her period in the leisure suite. Apparently her radio had drained of power; I wondered why I could not make contact earlier. She said parts of the place seemed a little unnerving but overall she felt there was no definite presence about.

Between 3.30 and 5.30 a.m. experiments with ultraviolet light photography, temperature sensors and electrostatic detectors were conducted. Faint dots of light were observed through the image intensifier with UV enhancement which was interesting. We found no temperature anomalies but sporadic drops and surges in electrostatic charge were noted, particularly in the reputedly haunted area of the auditorium. For the next two hours proceedings took on a very relaxed mood with only the fittest staying awake. Some of the staff had been up for twenty hours and would start work again shortly after the event ended at 8 a.m. – they did not appear enthusiastic at the prospect. Paula went over her Electronic Voice Phenomenon (EVP) experiments on the laptop and found nothing unusual. She still looked as fresh as a daisy and had lost no enthusiasm at all. The kit was packed away and we all sat sipping our final coffees.

Barry arrived at 7.45 a.m. and was as cheerful as ever, 'Did anyone see anything then?' The ghost had not put in an appearance but no one was complaining. It was an interesting night that raised £500 for the Variety Club. We wandered out bleary-eyed into a typical cold and grey November morning.

A follow-up visit was arranged by Paula for the next January. This would be more in-depth and involve a large number of observers, psychics, experimenters and photographers. Barry would attend this much shorter study from 11 p.m.. until 2 a.m..

American EVP expert, Linda Tweed, would work with Paula on trying to obtain evidence of paranormal voices as well as ultraviolet light filming. From the outset tests no temperature or electrostatic field anomalies were found. However, the radios yet again malfunctioned! We did find a rather bemusing carry-on on the large first floor foyer. The door leading to the ladies' toilet would periodically open a few inches with the most eerie creaking sound. After a while it would close again. It was a typical 'haunted house' creak and caused much amusement. It was probably caused by a mild draught but it never occurred on the previous event.

Hathern-based investigator Louise Tooley thought she saw someone on the staircase and assumed it was one of the investigative party. She asked who it was but received no response, she then trained a torch on the staircase but there was no one there.

For the last hour nearly the entire party converged into the haunted auditorium where several odd events did occur. Video cameras mysteriously drained of power, some torches also. There were a series of cool moving waves reported and some strange lights seen. Two of the persons present commented on 'tingling sensations' and felt slightly nauseous.

When all the data was gone over there were no EVPs or anything caught on any of the video cameras. It would be two years before I remembered the film I had in my camera at the cinema. When it was returned from processing there was one exposure taken in the main lobby where a strange pink haze is evident. Is it the ghost of Isabella Newell or simply a glitch? I suppose we will never know.

Harborough Theatre

Although only a few cinemas have a ghost or two, a large percentage of theatres do. One may ponder why as they both hold an audience captive. Might it be that living persons on the stage generate a more intense mood which in turn is absorbed by an audience then somehow provides the atmosphere in which psychic manifestations draw off? Of

Harborough Theatre. What must be a very palatial cycle shed harbours a psychic reminder of a long past evil deed.

course some theatres merely occupy an earlier site where the usual criteria for haunting phenomena may have originated.

Perhaps this is the case for the little Harborough Theatre in Church Square, Market Harborough. The building is deceptive as on first impression it appears as a well-preserved structure from the mid-eighteenth century. The building was in fact constructed as a rather grand bicycle shed for the large Symington's factory (now the council offices) in 1934. The site was originally occupied by an inn called The Green Dragon.

The busy little theatre now flourishes, hosting regular amateur dramatic productions and various social events. The theatre is run by keen volunteers who cover various functions: actors, dressers, carpenters, stagehands, scene shifters, box office staff and whatever else needs to be done.

Two volunteers, Viv, and her daughter-in-law, Ann, were busy doing some cleaning and organising one hot July day in 1989. Ann was in the claustrophobic wardrobe store under the seats of the auditorium, while Viv was using a vacuum cleaner just outside. Above the whine of the machine, Viv heard someone walking about above them. The footsteps emanated from the timber floor behind the back row. They were the only persons in the building, no one could have passed Viv in the narrow corridor and, anyway, the area was locked and in darkness. It then came about that Ann had also heard the footsteps and had assumed them to be Viv, who was out of sight at the time.

The mysterious footsteps were heard again one evening from a man in the sound and lighting box at the rear of the auditorium. It was in here where another anomaly presented itself. The sound engineer had taken delivery of a new tape of incidental music. He decided to run some of it to test the quality. Shortly into the recording there were undoubtedly human voices audible but making no sense. The perplexed sound man played the segment again but this time there was no such noise! Shortly after this event there were several instances when the internal communication system malfunctioned.

There was believed to be a sea captain living at the Green Dragon who died under mysterious circumstances. It is held widely that the old sea dog haunts the site, although why someone so beloved of the briny would live so far inland remains a mystery!

Another story concerns a maid at the inn. Her name was Hannah and she lived in, occupying a small room upstairs. She was stunningly beautiful and well aware of the fact. She liked to flirt with the men folk who would flock to the inn. She had a boyfriend called John, a young baker who was devoted to her but strongly disapproved of her flirty activities and sometimes would become very jealous. One night after closing time they had a violent argument. The next day John left the town and Hannah was never seen again.

Gossip soon got around that John had murdered Hannah in a fit of rage. A few weeks later this rumour was strengthened when a female body was discovered in the River Welland in a weir some ten miles from the town. Might it be the tragic ghost of flirty Hannah who wanders the theatre?

In the spring of 2004, public relations and media consultant Simon Sheikh began setting up an idea for raising funds for a national charity. In 1994 he had set up a night ghost hunt in Tutbury Castle that had been a huge success. With all the 'reality' shows seemingly taking over television some sort of spoof idea eventually came to light, so 'I'm a

Student, Get me Out of Here' was born. The format would be would be a small number of students being housed overnight in a haunted building. At some point they would be left alone in the dark to see how they fared. If the individual found the experience too much, the 'chicken switch' would be the phrase, 'I'm a student, get me out of here'. Various local businesses would sponsor the event to raise money.

Simon eventually decided on the Harborough Theatre and lost no time in approaching the company with the idea. Provisional confirmation was cleared and a date set for August.

Throughout June and July much planning was necessary. I was told of the event by a work colleague and thought to get involved in some way. I contacted Simon and was soon on board.

To add a sardonic twist the event took place on Friday 13th of August. I would go over on the train around 7 p.m.. I had quite a busy day – among other things I had to take one of my ferrets to the vet and pick it up in the late afternoon so I was denied the all important afternoon doze; it would be a miracle if I made it through the night.

While at Leicester's London Road railway station in the bar I received a telephone call from Mike Eason. The event was in the local press and Mike had read about it. We would meet up later in the town. I then boarded the train. It was a pleasant sunny evening as I idly gazed out. I particularly like the short journey from Leicester to Market Harborough. I had with me my cowhide shoulder bag with a few accoutrements, video camera, 35mm still camera, trifield meter (used for measuring electrostatic fields) and the obligatory snacks in the form of crisps, sweets, etc.

Charity event organiser, Mr Walker, met me at the station for the short journey into town. After a short photo shoot we all went into the theatre. The participants were Carol Slark, Nick Phillips, Leanne and Ann Battista; Simon of course would be running things. The event was to run for a twelve-hour period commencing at 8 p.m.. I however was given special dispensation and would soon go out into the town for a pub meal.

A sunny, warm Friday evening in a market town with unexplored pubs, sheer paradise! Unfortunately I was not to get my meal but met Mike Eason in the Sugarloaf, a Wetherspoons hostelry. I had not seen Mike for seven or eight years. He said I look younger as I get older! I was not feeling particularly young; perhaps it was the low light in the place. Mike gave me a copy of his short film *Haunted Harborough*. Was it really nine years since I contributed to this project? The gaiety was interrupted by the whine of my mobile telephone, could I get myself back? Alexander Graham Bell has a lot to answer for. With much chagrin I returned to the theatre, time to do some work.

The first of several radio interviews had been arranged by Simon. Once this was out of the way I went for a wander about. On the stage everything was set up for a forthcoming production, a typical suburban living room. The set reminded me of the scenes for the Mike Leigh classic comedy, *Abigail's Party*. I tested the floorboards at the rear of the auditorium, they creaked quite audibly. The place seemed quite serene with no eerie sensations; my scalp tends to tingle if I sense anything that may be of a psychic nature.

The café was the base room. Everyone was quaffing coffee and a feeling of cheerful anticipation filled the air. Mr Quinn, the theatre co-ordinator popped in to see how we were; he added that either himself or one of the other members of the company might drop in at some point before the 8 a.m. conclusion. Carol was sent out to find a takeaway and orders were taken; I could not be trusted to go out as the pubs were still open! My role in this event was merely to be on hand if required, help out if anyone became traumatised and boost moral. I would also do some infrared filming at intermittent periods throughout the night.

Two more radio interviews after midnight then the lights went out and we found a suitable place to sit or stand. Simon's endless enthusiasm caused friction with Leanne and a row broke out. I did a bit of peacemaking then suggested yet another coffee break. Tiredness and nerves can often lead to frayed tempers. I nipped off and did some filming in the dark auditorium and then some sundry tests for electrostatic surges that proved fruitless.

Nick found the area around the upper part of the upper staircase was slightly odd but no one else felt the place to be in any way ghostly. We did get one or two ghostly screams from passing drunks at around 2.30 a.m. though.

At around 3.45 a.m. I decided a doze was in order. Where better than lying on the carpet on the back row of the auditorium where the ghost walks? The whole place was now deathly silent; I think everyone was dozing somewhere about.

I was jolted awake by approaching footsteps which belonged to Leanne and Nick. Everyone, except me, had reached the level of lethargy that sleep deprivation brings so the youngest of those present decided to keep mobile rather than succumb. They mentioned that another of the theatre people popped in a while ago, an Italian-looking man, while there he did a few jobs in the kitchen.

The dawn came and we all retired to the café for the last hour or so. Mr Quinn arrived at 7.20 a.m. and seems pleased that the place was in good order. Carol and Ann had cleaned the café up earlier, thankfully!

Well, the immortal words, 'I'm a student, get me out of here' was never uttered but an interesting twist to the proceedings came when Simon mentioned the Italian-looking man who came by at around 5 a.m... Mr Quinn seemed quite puzzled by this as no one else had visited and the description given was not familiar at all!

Battlefields

Ancient battlefields exist all over England. Leicestershire has several such sites, including Ankle Hill in Melton Mowbray where a very bloody battle took place in 1645 and the famous Battle of Bosworth, fought in 1485.

The Bosworth site near Sutton Cheney has preserved its heritage and the visitor has plenty of historic information on hand. Every year here one may view a re-enactment of the battle and perhaps get a feel of the terrible skirmish that took place on 22 August 1485.

It was on an eve of such a re-enactment in 1997 that a small party arrived near dusk at a pub in Sutton Cheney for a quick beer or two before going on to the site as there are said to be ghosts here. The idea was to see if the atmosphere created by the preparations and the volume of re-enactors may in some way evoke dormant psychic influences. The pub was half-full of semi-drunken men and women already dressed for the occasion and later on it was surreal to view costumed characters wandering along the side of the road.

Wally Wilford knew the area and where our eventual positions of observation would be. When we arrived the car park was nearly half-full. There was little moonlight so in almost total darkness we got out the kit bags which for a job like this contain torches, cameras, flasks and sandwiches. Although temperatures were typical for late August, it would get chilly later on so we had thick coats to carry as well. After gauging the vicinity of where the cars were parked so they could be later found we trudged off into the gloom. At one point we observed the spectacle of a vast number of tents illuminated by large campfires. There was much merriment in the air as groups of re-enactors partook in various alcoholic concoctions. A compass may have been useful as we were going around in circles. Eventually it was deemed necessary to ask for help, we approached a group of re-enactors. A minor indiscretion by Alex made me wince, 'Oh, we're just common or garden ghost hunters'. The braying group saw us on our way. I had a sneaking suspicion high jinks would be on the cards later on.

After a seemingly endless trek we found the little station of the Cadeby Light Railway, we crossed over then along the canal which led to a track through a copse into a small area with picnic tables – ideal. Wally was satisfied this would be the position for the duration of the observation. Would the phantom white horse put in an appearance, or the headless figure reported in the vicinity?

At just after midnight murmurings and stifled laughter heralded the first 'ghost' of the night. A character in a long red garment and an odd-looking hat climbed over a fence and to the accompaniment of his hidden friends, leapt into view and performed a quite splendid somersault. The unseen ones provided a repertoire of eerie wails as the 'ghost' ran into the gloom. The audience of deadpan ghost hunters obligingly applauded hoping this would be the first and last of the entertainment. It would not be.

Apart from what looked like a greyish, silent figure observed by Sue and I that was a mystery as it simply came and went, the night settled to uneventful silence. If nothing else it was a pleasant experience with a valuable lesson: always use your discretion.

An enactment of a different kind was experienced here in the early 1980s. As a coach-load of passengers alighted by a field, and one lady felt particularly ill at ease. The event was a steam rally on a sunny August afternoon with all the noise, excitement and joviality of such an event. The huge beasts displaying their prowess as proud owners and envious enthusiasts chatted while the crowds meandered.

The lady seemed unaware of any of the atmosphere, she was in another dimension. To her it was not warm and sunny but cold and grey. It was not long before her friends noticed her detached state. She started to talk about 'the hill' and slowly began to show signs of intense distress. Her friends, who were clearly confused, tried in vain to console her. Their concern was then increased as the lady asked them to bring her a horse as the hill was only a short gallop away.

The scene was now a dark hell. Sounds of shouting and terrible screaming filled the air as the lady shivered. She heard the clashing of steel and dreadful moans. Then, suddenly she was back to where she should be; the living nightmare just ceased leaving her very shaken as her friends consoled her.

Anyone with an interest in the world of steam will be familiar with the late Reverend Edward (Teddy) Boston. His tireless enthusiasm and huge collection of model steam engines were held in awe. His beloved Cadeby Light Railway was in his parish of All Saints' Church in Cadeby. He was also well aware of the geography of Bosworth Field, being an enthusiastic member of the Richard III Society.

He had organised this steam rally and when the strange episode with the lady reached him he put forward a most interesting, if unnerving explanation. The 'hill' the lady seemed obsessed with must have been Ambion Hill where the battle itself took place on that fateful day. The day of the battle was unseasonably cold and grey like the lady experienced. To cap it all, the day of her experience was on the 22 August, the anniversary.

A similar incident occurred in 1949 at the site of the Battle of Naseby, just over in Northamptonshire, fought in 1645. A young couple on a cycling trip decided to rest up on a bridle path in a cornfield. It was mid-June, oppressively hot, humid and still. Anyone who cycles will know that in such heat, a feeling of almost being poached sets in when one stops. They sat in the shade of a haystack drinking warm lemonade when a feeling of expectancy filled the air, and it seemed deadly silent. Then, silent figures simply appeared from nowhere. The astonished couple stared as the dust-streaked figures pulled and pushed wooden carts, some with chains banging mutely against the sides. Some of the figures wore dark leather jerkins and high boots, their overall appearance was unkempt. Soon the figures and carts faded into nothingness leaving two flabbergasted observers.

It would be several days before the couple learned that their bizarre experience had occurred on the anniversary of the battle, 14 June.

* * * *

In the mid-1950s an Ashby de la Zouch man was out on an evening walk. He was on Corkscrew Lane near Coleorton. Passing a copse, he became aware of an awful din, with agonising screams, clashing of metal, and horses neighing. The man stopped and peered through the gaps in the trees but saw nothing at all. To him, the dreadful noise sounded like an ancient battle. The sounds faded after a minute or two. The man felt uncomfortable and unwilling to remain, and moved away with renewed spring in his step.

The man spoke to one or two people about the mystery and it was soon established he was not the only one to have heard the sounds. It later came to light that a violent clash had taken place near the copse during the Civil War.

* * * *

A few years ago I received an interesting contact from a Leicestershire man. His account is quite short but worthy of mention. In the late 1990s, the man and his son were out in a large, ploughed field near Newton Harcourt. It was a pleasant, mild evening. They were treasure-hunting with a metal detector. Suddenly the device was wrenched from the man and flew several feet. They stared open-mouthed at each other as a dramatic change in the atmosphere set in as if a thunderstorm was building up. Then both saw, fleetingly, a large number of figures. The only feature they recalled later was that the figures had shining metal helmets.

From our discussion and my suggestions, the man agreed that there might have been bodies buried under the ground, maybe even Romans. The 'warning' to leave well alone was heeded and the pair gave that area of land a wide berth!

* * * *

The sprawling Wigston Harcourt housing estate has spread out along the old A50 up to Cooks Lane where for decades there used to be old railway carriages in a small holding. Opposite the large cemetery is a traffic island onto Guthlaxton Way leading to Heards Close, an average suburban cul-de-sac.

Part of the estate is built on a field that was called Heards Close. This patch of land had a sinister reputation. In 1981, before the houses were built, a woman and her young son spent two nights on the field in their caravan. Their car had developed problems. The repairs would take a couple of days so their caravan was towed out to the field. The garage owner would bring them back once the work was done.

The next morning a curious local resident came over and soon got chatting to the woman who explained that she had had a terrible night. Loud cries, awful moaning sounds and what sounded like sword fighting had woken her. It sounded like she was in the middle of a violent battle.

The second morning the resident came over again to see how the caravan dwellers had fared. Slightly better, no battle sounds but she suddenly awoke and sat bolt upright as the words, 'Get Up' were shouted in a childish voice. It was her son, what was up? In the gloom she saw a boy wearing a whitish garment, he looked cadaverous. The child then vanished. She was then relieved to see her son sleeping soundly. She felt that the place was evil. Later in the day they left the site with much relief.

In 1880 when the cemetery was put to use, gravediggers discovered myriad items such as broken shields, bits of armour and remains of swords, also a number of skeletons. Some have suggested that the ancient artefacts may be from AD 876 when the Danes pillaged Wigston.

Not so long after the business on Heards Close a resident was at the kitchen sink of her home on Horsewell Lane. She idly gazed out over the mist-blanketed cemetery when she observed a curious vision. Many hazy figures appeared that seemed to be marching. They had some kind of armour and were carrying spears or long swords. Before she could believe her eyes, the entire vision faded just leaving the misty cemetery.

Papillon Hall

We have all seen the films and televised adaptations of a haunting in a gloomy mansion. There is nearly always a portrait that affects the heroine in some way and more often than not it would have a hypnotic effect and emanate evil. The ghost would always be found to be the person in the portrait. There would be the obligatory skeleton found in a bricked up room and perhaps even a curse. These are the ingredients of a good ghost story – pure fiction of course, hardly likely to happen in reality. Or could they?

Papillon Hall. A typical haunted house full of mystery.

Papillon Hall was built in 1622. It stood nearly a mile west of Lubenham. Stoutly built of stone, the hall was south-facing and of octagonal design. It had a moat and a secret passage to the River Welland. The roofs were designed in the shape of a cross formed by the gables with lead flats facing south-west and south-east, and the other two roofs accessed by attics. It is thought the design was for the placement of cannon. The land on which the hall was built used to be part of Leicester Abbey and there was a spring in the grounds known as St Mary's Well.

David Papillon, who built the hall, died on 18 March 1659. The hall stayed with the family until 1764 when it was purchased by William Stevens. There was a succession of owners until the eventual destruction of the building in 1950.

The first indication of a haunting came in December 1866. Lord Hopetown had acquired the hall and, shortly after taking possession, the family were subjected to a barrage of unexplained bumps and bangs echoing about the corridors.

Little heed had been paid to the village gossip of a curse in the house. Apparently a pair of green and silver brocade slippers were never to

Pamp. A portrait that has hypnotic and evil influences.

leave the hall. If the shoes were disturbed, those foolhardy enough to interfere would be cursed and subjected to torment from a discarnate source. After one particularly bad night of upheaval, the family decided to look into the story of the cursed shoes.

It was discovered that the slippers dated from around 1730. The third David of the Papillon dynasty, known as 'Pamp' or 'Old Pamp' or 'Lord Pamp', married Mary Keyser in 1717. He had a mistress, thought to be of Spanish origin, who was never allowed to leave the house. She vanished under mysterious circumstances; the slippers were believed to have been hers. The legend then came about that the slippers were cursed and to remain within the confines of Papillon Hall.

Lord Hopetown consulted the rector of Lubenham on the matter. He was informed that the previous owner had bequeathed everything (including the slippers) to his daughter. Lord Hopetown then set about finding the benefactor who was soon located in Leicester and the slippers were recovered.

This seemed to pacify the mysterious noises and nocturnal upheaval about the place. After a few years Papillon Hall was sold to Thomas Halford on 17 October 1872.

The Halfords were fascinated by the superstition around the slippers but took no notice of the supposed curse. They decided to pack them up and have them sent over to France for the Paris Exhibition, as with their dubious history they would make an interesting exhibit.

The Halfords were then to incur the wrath of the curse as a gamut of violent noises around the house became quite intolerable. Things became so bad that the family attempted to get the slippers back but as a registered exhibit they would remain for the duration of the year-long exhibition. The Halfords could not put up with the atmosphere and Papillon Hall was sold once again.

The next occupier, Mr C.W. Walker, was less cynical of such ideas and took the matter seriously. He even had a special iron safe built for the preservation of the slippers; the small box was fitted over the hall fireplace. After many pleasant and undisturbed years, the hall was sold on to Captain Frank Belville in 1903.

Captain Belville threw scorn on the legend and defiantly had the slippers transferred to his solicitor's offices. There would be some major changes to Papillon Hall.

Renowned architect, Sir Edward Lutyens, was commissioned to carry out the renovations. A third floor would be added. This work required the demolition of one of the attic rooms. It was during this stage that a skeleton was discovered in a small, walled-up room. The skeleton was later established to be that of a female. The local builders were less than happy as rumours spread that the slippers belonging to whoever had been bricked up. This unrest increased dramatically when one of the builders was struck by a falling brick then later died as a result. Eventually all the men flatly refused to have anything to do with the place so work was halted while another firm was contracted; these were from well out of the locality.

To have a respite from the chaos, Captain Belville took his wife out in the pony trap to have lunch with friends in Market Harborough. Shortly into the journey the pony bolted, the trap tipped over and they both fell out. The Captain sustained a severe blow to the head but lived; his wife luckily escaped unhurt.

The slippers were swiftly returned to the house. They were placed in a glass casket and put on a side table in the parlour. Then further trouble ensued. While hunting, the Captain sustained a fractured skull. As a result a metal plate had to be inserted. Then shortly after this a violent thunderstorm struck the hall and stables, killing a groom, a hunter and three ponies.

During the Second World War the building was occupied by detachments of the US 82nd Airborne Division. It was not long before the 'Yanks' found out about the legend. One small group led by one particularly foolish private took away one of the slippers. The private died soon after. The others decided to put the thing back. Some weeks later, two of the detachment removed a single slipper. They were both killed during the Nijmegen air drop in 1944. The dreaded slipper apparently found itself back where it belonged.

In September 1950, Mrs Barbara Papillon and her sister-in-law, Muriel Tindall, visited the empty hall. The place was eerie and dilapidation was abundant. Up in the open safe was one slipper and patten, a shoe with a raised sole for muddy conditions. They contacted the head of the demolition company and asked if they might have the remaining slipper. He could not care less. Miraculously the other slipper was discovered under floorboards later into the demolition. Today, the slippers are retained in Leicester Museum.

The sinister influence that pervaded the hall was believed to be Pamp. He was very charismatic and unnerved many with his hypnotic stare. He claimed to be psychic which added to the uneasiness he often seemed to exude – a mysterious character indeed.

It is said he could 'fix' people with his hypnotic powers. There is one tale of Pamp being less than pleased with the efforts of two hands ploughing a field. He trudged over to the two men and hypnotised them into a static condition like a pair of mannequins. They were left like this for the remainder of the day then Pamp 'released' them, they were none the worse for their experience.

Locally he was loathed and feared. He was considered by some as a jinx. If anything bad happened in the village, it would be the work of Pamp.

No one quite knows a lot about the mysterious Spanish lady Pamp kept hidden at the hall. Apparently her only exercise was wandering the flat lead roofs after dark. All that is certain is that she was hidden away in an attic room, later known as 'Pamp's Attic', the room where the skeleton was discovered.

A portrait of Pamp affected several people. It would transfix some who beheld it. Some found the picture to be evil and exude menace, the eyes would follow you. There were beliefs that the portrait was haunted and that Pamp would 'form' in the picture, leave its confines and wander the hall.

One servant girl was disturbed from her slumber by a series of odd sounds in the bedroom not unlike the scratching of a cat on a nocturnal prowl. The wench, in a state of agitation, reached down and found one of her shoes then threw it in the direction of the animal. But it was no cat. Standing at the end of the bed was a man dressed exactly as the portrait of Pamp, even his dandified wig stood out in the moonlight.

The portrait itself was painted in 1715 and depicts David Papillon at the age of twenty-four. Shortly after his marriage he left the hall to reside at Acrise Place in Kent. He died in 1762 aged seventy-one.

There had been regular reports of awful wailing sounds around the building and fleeting sightings of a mysterious apparition believed to be David Papillon. The most enduring account concerns the experiences of a Mrs Bertha Tufnell. At the end of the nineteenth century Pelham Rawstorn Papillon was living at Crowhurst Park near Hastings. The then owner of Papillon Hall, C.W. Walker, let the property with all its furnishings – including the portrait of Pamp – to Colonel Tufnell and his wife, Bertha. Soon after both Colonel and Mrs Tufnell noticed an uneasy feeling around the picture. Occasional visitors would remark on the portrait and some became obsessed with it. They would spend long periods simply staring at the eyes. The governess had a particular dislike of it and one evening she became so upset by the thing that Mrs Tufnell told her to go up to her room. The governess claimed that 'it' followed her upstairs into her room. This was later to be found that others including guests had experienced this unpleasant feeling.

One afternoon Mrs Tufnell was entertaining a few friends in the drawing room. She observed a faint misty cloud form near to one visitor, Mrs Muriel Tindall, née Papillon. Slowly the hazy mist formed into a vertical column then colour and features began to appear. Soon the clear apparition of Pamp manifested. The figure was dressed as in the portrait. It was obvious that Mrs Tindall was unaware of the vision. Admirably, Mrs Tufnell somehow managed to retain her composure during the appearance. Later, when reflecting on the experience, Mrs Tufnell thought that Pamp looked pleased, perhaps as one of his descendants was present.

The mist appeared many times after, always in the drawing room. Mrs Tufnell would hastily quote a common prayer which seemed to restrict the mist from developing into a full-blown, solid apparition.

Her sister-in-law became quite obsessed with the portrait. She would be transfixed by the impassive Pamp, staring at it for ages. Mrs Tufnell had to physically remove her from it on one occasion. Without doubt, the image was unhealthy and influenced certain people.

Mrs Tufnell wrote a letter to Pelham Rawstorn Papillon telling of her disquiet and asked of the possibility that the offending portrait be removed. This request was granted. He arranged for the portrait to be taken to his Hastings residence. Employees at the Crowhurst Park estate, Mr and Mrs Pettit would arrange the carrier and build a suitable crate for its transition to their cottage on the Hastings to Battle road. On the night of the arrival of the portrait, Mr Pettit accidentally drowned in the well.

The portrait was eventually housed in Pelham Rawstorn Papillon's bedroom in Hastings. Another artefact would reside with it. In September 1908, Pelham was visited by Mr C.W. Walker, who had sold Papillon Hall to Captain Belville. He explained that he had in his possession an old square stone. Apparently the slab had been used as a cover on the well at Papillon Hall. Pamp called it 'an everlasting well', a magic well with healing powers. The stone had at one time borne the Papillon coat of arms. Ever since he took up residence at Holmhurst, Burwash, in Sussex he had been plagued with bad luck and a series of misfortunes. He could not say for definite that the relic was in any way connected but begged Pelham to take possession of the stone. The request was duly granted and a few days later the slab arrived and was put under the bed. Pelham reported no misfortunes or anything else unusual while in possession of the two articles.

Papillon Hall was, however, still a place where inexplicable happenings would continue. George Atherton, the butler to the next owner, Captain Belville, reported two peculiar incidents. He was sitting down playing cards with the chauffeur when there was an almighty crash in the scullery. They both leapt up and ran over expecting to find broken china everywhere; but there was nothing out of place whatsoever. The other incident was late one evening, George had just retired. As he climbed into bed he heard a loud noise. He put on the light and saw the window was broken. He went over and peered outside but saw nothing or no one. Puzzled, George again retired. Next morning it was discovered by one of the housemaids that George's bedroom chair was broken. It then came to light that a sizeable piece of the chair had been found on the lawn below the broken window.

After the war the hall stood empty despite attempts to sell the property. Papillon Hall sadly deteriorated to a perilous condition before its demolition. In 1988, a local man who as a child had been told of 'the old haunted house' decided to visit the site of Papillon Hall. On arriving he was surprised at how much still remained: an entire perimeter wall, a run down summerhouse, the stables and part of the courtyard. Further probing revealed the remains of the 'magic well' and the wine cellar with the rusted iron racks still in-situ.

As a result, BBC Radio Leicester did an outside broadcast on the land with the man and the owners of the farm which stood on the site. The occupier mentioned that there was an uneasiness about the place and strange noises had been heard coming from the stables. They all then visited the stables. It was here that a segment of tape somehow wiped itself clean; it had to be re recorded. When the tape was later spliced for editing the sounds of a child crying was audible in the background. This was a total mystery.

This prompted further delving. Where were the notorious slippers and the portrait? After months of painstaking research the man found one descendant who had his property pertaining to Papillon Hall bequeathed to the Leicestershire Museum Trust. No time was lost setting an appointment to view some of the artefacts, including the slippers.

The meeting was set for 2 p.m.. The man and a colleague were there promptly but where was the archivist? Almost an hour later, the archivist turned up. She appeared to be somewhat distraught. Apparently, shortly into her journey to the museum she became aware of a dog, a stray, following her. The animal remained with her then for no apparent reason attacked the woman; the dog then ran off. Luckily her wounds were minor and did not require hospital treatment. As well as viewing the slippers, the two men perused some of the myriad documents. One letter was of much interest as it centred on what might have been the last demonstration of hypnotism by Pamp. They were then told that the driver who brought some of the items 'lost' three hours! The journey from Colchester normally was three hours, the dazed driver could not account for the remainder, the 'lost hours'.

The final piece of the man's hard efforts was to track down the old retainer, George Atherton. Although ailing, George recalled the haunting with full clarity and spoke of his experiences as very real and terrifying.

If travelling towards Lubenham from the west, look out for a tree-lined avenue, all that remains of Papillon Hall.

As we close the chapter on Papillon Hall we must be proud to have had a classic ghost story within Leicestershire. As for the portrait, who knows? It might be somewhere in the Home Counties, if it is hanging, those who behold it would be prudent to show caution and let Pamp remain within his portrait.

One offs

There are instances where a ghost will be experienced just once. This is interesting in that the integrity of the witness may be questionable in some cases but not all. There are indeed some 'hauntings' that are a result of misinterpretation and suggestion. The 'ghost' may be anything from a cloud of gnats to a mere trick of the light and may be so convincing that local word will spread and a haunting will be created. I will present some that are believed to be of genuine origin. The old lodge in Abbey Park is reputedly haunted but the ruins of Cavendish House are not. However, an unusual incident occurred amongst the ruins. It concerns a short exchange of words between a gardener and a man dressed in Elizabethan clothing. This is most unusual as it is most rare for an apparition to speak. The man was most interested in Cavendish House and spoke enthusiastically. The gardener assumed him to be an actor, perhaps for an open air pageant in the park. Only when the man promptly vanished did the gardener realise he had been chatting to a ghost. Nothing was reported before this incident in the mid-1970s or since.

*****

The little church of St Wistan's in Wigston Magna, on the busy Bull Head Street has no haunted reputation. However a couple wandering around the churchyard were staggered to confront a weird figure like a hologram. Another couple sharing an umbrella one rainy evening in 1994 were hastily walking along Peacock Lane in Leicester. They noticed a very tall man in front wearing a green floppy hat and long coat. He was only a few yards ahead when he turned into New Street.

When the couple arrived at the junction they looked over but he had gone.

A barmaid being driven home after a night stint at the Crows Nest pub on Glenfield Road saw a strange sight. As the car approached Bow Bridge she noticed a solitary figure which took her interest. She then realised it was a robed and hooded monk. On looking back the figure vanished.

In 1918 several villagers witnessed a greyish figure in Markfield. It was evening as the spectre was observed gliding through the cemetery. The very same figure was seen later on near to the cemetery. It was more formed and described as a woman.

In June 1935 a groom was leading two horses past Mount St Bernard's Abbey in Charnwood. It was a pleasant summer afternoon and he had just passed the large main gates when he saw one of the monks in a white habit standing by the side of the road. As the groom drew nearer the monk slowly levitated upwards then glided along the high stone wall before slowly vanishing. The groom was of course shocked and the horses became seriously affected. A while later the groom happened to read an article in a newspaper and discovered that one of the monks, Brother Finbar Holland, had been in the pump house which was behind the high wall and had suddenly died there. This happened earlier on the day of the experience.

One very morning in 1975 an electrical appliance engineer was on his way to Twycross. He was driving along the B4116. At the crossroads with the B586 near Measham he stopped. The road was clear apart from a cyclist laboriously approaching the junction. In fact the cyclist, a man wearing a raincoat and a flat cap was so slow the engineer was getting a bit impatient. At last he passed, the driver then looked both ways and was stunned to notice the cyclist had vanished into thin air.

These one-off experiences are all outdoors. There are one-off appearances inside houses that are usually classed as 'crisis apparitions' and are familiar as relatives or friends of those who perceive them. If instead of these singular appearances or a visitations there are further appearances then they can be classified as hauntings.

Harlaxton Manor. A most enigmatic and foreboding place.

Harlaxton Manor

This book is mostly concerned with haunted Leicestershire but I feel justified to encroach a few miles north-east of the boundary into Lincolnshire as it has a rather splendid haunted pile.

Many years ago I was on a coach trip on its way back from Lincolnshire. Just as dusk was setting we were given the cheerful news that the coach would be stopping at the Gregory Arms, thank heavens! Just as the coach slowed down to turn in I noticed some high turrets poking above the trees. What was this place? I asked my partner, Sue, to get the drinks while I just nipped along the road to look at something. I strolled along the verge then crossed over to a gatehouse and stared at this magnificent, well, palace. In the mauve sky of an August dusk the place was deathly silent with a haunting quality. I had a camera on the coach but the place was about a mile from the road and it was too dark. A breathtaking sight, would the place be haunted? It deserved to be. As the coach later drew away I craned my neck to look back and was rewarded to glimpse parts of the structure which was now floodlit, it looked like pure gold.

I discovered from a map that the place was called Harlaxton Manor. Further digging revealed that work started on the building in the late 1820s and that it took over twenty years to build. A Mr Gregory (which explains the name of the pub) who had it built to house his vast collection of fine art. Unfortunately he died before the manor was completed.

It passed through the Gregory family until 1938 when it was purchased by Mrs Violet Van-der-Elst. This rich and formidable woman soon began to make changes to the pile, including calling it Harlaxton Castle. Over twenty miles of cables brought electrical services to all of the hundred large rooms and new plumbing was installed – a massive undertaking.

After her husband's death she became fascinated with spiritualism. She would spend many evenings in the library conducting séances to contact her dead husband. Obviously the grief was intense as large black curtains were fitted and many black furnishings were introduced. She herself wore black for much of the time until her death in 1966.

She was remembered for her humanitarian beliefs and had campaigned for the abolition of the death penalty. Her brushless shaving cream business had earned her the fortune to posses Harlaxton Manor, otherwise known as Grantham Castle.

If anyone would linger and haunt this vast pile it would indeed be Violet Van der Elst, and yes, on many occasions a silent, dark, robed figure has been beheld in the library and a tangible presence has permeated much of the house. When it was acquired by Jesuits in 1948 the unsettled atmosphere was considered so intense, they conducted a series of exorcisms.

Harlaxton Manor was then owned by Stamford University for several years before passing onto the University of Evansville. It was initially a study centre then later the British campus, known as Harlaxton College, and remains so to this day.

Ghost enthusiasts may recognise Harlaxton Manor was used for location on the 1998 remake of the 1963 classic, *The Haunting*. As a point of interest, although the film is set in America, Ettington Park in Warwickshire was the house in the earlier film and both locations are around forty miles from Leicester.

I made an unsuccessful attempt to spend a night at Harlaxton Manor. I received an invitation to visit in the day during term time. However, working in a university, as I do, I thought this less than ideal. To get the benefit of somewhere like this I would need to quietly wander alone the endless corridors in the dead of night.

There may be more than one phantom at Harlaxton. There is a sad tale of a nursery maid holding a baby before a large fire. Not only did she rock the baby to sleep, but dozed off herself. The baby fell into the fire and died horribly. This story may be questionable but more than one visitor has commented on the screams and the sounds of an infant crying. A vase was once seen to lift then float in mid-air and a greyish apparition was seen in the blue corridor. The most dramatic incident must be the hazy outline of a large man that appeared in the doorway of the library. Not only did a lecturer observe it but several students. The thing remained in view for nearly ten minutes before fading out.

Whilst perusing the alumni recollections of former students it seems clear that no one has any bad memories of Harlaxton. They recall drunken evenings in the Gregory Arms, the 'naked mile' (a tradition of running the mile-long drive in the nude), semi-drunken 'ghost hunts' in the haunted clock room and bell tower at Hallowe'en, and the general atmosphere of the magnificent building. Some recall the almost nightly experience of just on the point of falling asleep, the foot of the bed being touched and patted as if someone was tucking them in. Interestingly no one would remember the sensation after or during the next day even; it would just come at the point of slumber. No one had any fear of it, if anything it was a comfort to many, being a long way from home.

The Opera House

There are, on occasion, cases where quite regular haunting phenomena go on but ceases the second those engaged in ghost research venture near. I recall many years ago a case in a hotel where supernatural disturbances were almost a daily occurrence. During my visits nothing ever happened. The perplexed manager would tell me things would happen almost seconds before my arrival and most often after my departure all hell would break loose!

My most recent case such as this was at the award-winning restaurant, The Opera House on Guildhall Lane, Leicester. Historian and Blue Badge guide, Virginia Wright contacted me in 2001 after Val Weafer, the proprietor, spoke to her of the ghostly goings on. I telephoned Val, we chatted for forty-five minutes before I arranged a preliminary visit.

The site has an interesting history. It is thought an inn existed here as early as the mid-fourteenth century. Later, the inn was converted into two cottages, numbers 10 and 12 Townhall Lane, as it was then known. In the mid-1770s, number 10 was turned into a pub, the

Queens Head Inn. In 1896 the site was converted into the Opera House Hotel. However the place developed something of a reputation as a house of ill-repute (in other words it was also a brothel) and closed after eighteen years. The sewing machine manufacturer Walter O' Brien Ltd occupied the premises for many years before Val and Noel Weafer bought the property. After some renovation work the restaurant opened its doors in 2000.

Shortly after the business became established, there would be the occasional feeling of 'something', an unsettling feeling. This was noticed mainly after serving on a busy evening, Saturdays in particular.

Over the weeks a tangible presence would unnerve the waitresses. This seemed mainly confined to the area of the building where 12 Townhall Lane existed. This part of the restaurant is called the Church Room as it offers views of St Martin's. Late one evening a waitress came to Val claiming to have glimpsed a shadowy figure in this room.

Sometimes Val would admit to feeling a little ill at ease when being last out after locking up late at night. On one occasion heard Val heard a rattling sound near the Church Room. Val eventually discovered the sound to be coming from a door that leads into a small yard. She stared dumbstruck as the metal latch twitched up and down totally unaided. A few months later a knife was seen to fall off a table in the Church Room. This happened several times and even a diner who saw it happen asked Val if the place was haunted!

On my short preliminary visit Val pointed out the areas of the building where it seemed a presence exists and the table where the knife incidents had occurred. Val put forward the idea that vibration from passing vehicles could be the cause for the knife falling off the table, a sensible idea but why just one of the tables? I checked that the table did not wobble. We also visited the sizeable cellars, also converted for eating. I suggested carrying out a series of observations after business finished on Saturdays. Val seemed keen on the idea so dates were set.

In total I introduced a total of twenty-seven researchers to the case over the coming months. Psychics, photographers, observers and specialists in one angle or another with various experiments conducted. The ghost staunchly refused to show up. However there was one curious incident in December 2002. A visiting psychic agreed to see what she could make of the affair. It was arranged for the psychic to arrive before opening time on a Thursday evening. I arranged to meet her. The lady would slowly wander the restaurant while I waited upstairs at the bar. On her return she mentioned the chap in the white shirt downstairs. I knew this to be the assistant manager who was bemused by all this ghost business. I told the psychic I knew all about him then asked for her overall impression. They were quite simple: 'culture shock': a totally harmless psychic remnant trying to come to terms with all the people, gaiety and general busy restaurant culture after a long period of quiet.

We then left; the psychic led me down St Martin's East where a monk regularly walks before moving through the churchyard of St Martin's. Unfortunately his essence was not about at this time. She added that the monk was well aware of the present and heartily disapproved!

Some weeks later I learned of an incident in the restaurant which threw a different light on the psychic's visit. Late on a Saturday evening, a couple were at the bar arranging to pay for their meal. Just as Val was sorting their bill, the lady moved aside so a man could get past. She looked around to see him vanish straight into a wall. No one else saw anything and Val was quite sympathetic and humorous. It then came to light that the man wore a white shirt!

Then word of another sighting reached Val. Someone approaching the restaurant observed a woman lurking in the doorway. As the witness casually wondered what the woman was doing she just vanished. There were then several instances of lone waitresses singing while clearing up hearing a loud, 'Sssshhh' into their ear from an invisible source. Val wonders if this is Mrs Kale who lived for many years in one of the cottages and was less than impressed with today's musical tastes.

The ghost hunter's job is not only to evaluate a case but try to calm and reduce activity. On this occasion we had failed as none of the personnel seemed to link in with any psychic manifestation. However, there was an unsettling episode one night towards the end of the studies. Val's son, Adam, stayed up with us and shortly after midnight he endured a strong influence which left him somewhat upset. I have seen similar situations before when a medium 'opens up' and draws in whatever energies exist; in some cases one is bombarded. I explained to Val that one of us should have been in line for something like that. The feelings of depression and desperation stayed with Adam for quite some time.

A clergyman offered to assist in 'moving on' the offending spirit or spirits but Val felt that no one had really come to any harm so for the moment she would tolerate the oddities that are now at least less regular.

The Three Swans

The Three Swans hotel in Market Harborough is reputedly haunted by one of its former innkeepers. It is the oldest inn in the town, dating back to the sixteenth century, and has also served for the town's petty sessions and meetings of town officials.

Mr John Fothergill bought the coaching inn in 1934. A meticulous character with a passion for silver buckled shoes, he was revered and possibly eccentric but kept an orderly house. His memoirs, *An Innkeeper's Diary'* is a rare classic of its type. There is a small lounge called the Fothergill Room which has a portrait and several framed press cuttings about him. The painting depicts Fothergill casting a stern demeanour, reflecting his formidable presence. Some think his presence still lingers. There are stories that any interference or removal of the portrait may result in an upsetting atmosphere building up and in some cases mysterious banging sounds and beer mugs flying off shelves.

One member of staff, Margaret, knows only too well of the haunting phenomena about the building. She remembers the family who stayed for a week in 1985. The man, his wife and two children took a large room overlooking the town. They were very pleased with the room but their Labrador dog would not enter the room at all; it spent the duration outside in the corridor. Two chambermaids told her of seeing a large lounge chair moving about unaided while cleaning this particular room. There was a chambermaid who died in 1994 who Margaret subsequently glimpsed around the upper rooms. She was most conscientious about her work and Margaret thinks she returns periodically to ensure her high standards are maintained. She may have been responsible for an incident that resulted in scaring a regular guest so badly that he never took that particular room on subsequent visits. The man was taking a shower when he was handed a sponge, he took the sponge then realised he was alone in the bathroom!

During the making of a local film, *Haunted Harborough*, the producer, Mike Eason, brought a medium to look at the inn. Ironically she detected a strong presence in the corridor where the Labrador felt at ease; in another area there was a strong impression of a young man. The man had committed suicide, was not place-centred and moved freely about. The housekeeper later confirmed that in the mid-1970s

The Three Swans Hotel, Market Harborough.
A former maid is said to linger here.

there was a member of staff, a young fellow of around 20 years of age, who had taken his own life but not in this part of the building.

The housekeeper took the medium and Mike to the area where the young man took his own life. The medium explained there was a strong feeling of his presence. Basically he had a drug dependency which had led to psychological problems and even schizophrenia. Additionally there were family problems, he could not cope and with a drug overdose took his own life.

So, there may be more than one phantom abroad in the Three Swans, yet another old coaching inn with its ghosts.

Bottesford

The 1949 feature film *Twelve O' Clock High* tells of the drama around an American airbase in England during the Second World War. Much of the focus is centred on a new commander (portrayed by Gregory Peck) who is a no-nonsense figure, fair but tough, determined to see this thing through, no matter what. His staunch character was ably supported by the wise but sympathetic Major Harvey Stovall (acted by Dean Jagger who, quite rightly, won an Academy Award). The mounting pressure of the level of bombing missions over Germany and

The phantom airman of Bottesford Airfield.

the morale of the exhausted crews slowly begin to eat away at the commander's character, and he starts to crack, just like his predecessor.

The opening and closing scenes of the film depict Major Harvey Stovall, returning to the airfield some years after the war. He wanders the overgrown airfield, the hangars, the dispersal bays and the control tower which was the hub of the operations. Everything is silent, just a slight breeze.

Many such airfields were created with much speed. At one stage there were ninety-three airfields in operation across England. A large majority of these occupied land in East Anglia and Lincolnshire where the flat conditions were ideal.

A number of the control towers survive today. They vary in size and are generally constructed from concrete block slabs with brick interior walls. They all had steel-framed doors and windows. The larger towers have a viewing balcony on all sides, otherwise the flat roof would have served this purpose. Some have been used for offices for commercial aviation, some are used for storing agricultural equipment and one or two have been converted into homes. The rest have simply stood abandoned for sixty years.

A quite significant number of these towers and airfields are reputedly haunted. I have visited some of the abandoned control towers. They do indeed harbour a certain atmosphere. As one slowly wanders the empty rooms, corridors and staircase it is easy to imagine the sights and sounds of when the tower was in operation, creating one's own ghosts. I have personally experienced nothing of a paranormal nature during my time in these places but that does not mean there were no ghosts.

At the northern tip of Leicestershire lies the village of Bottesford. Quite near stand the buildings left from the old RAF base. It opened as a military airfield in 1941 and closed at the end of the war in 1945. As well as the RAF, it was home to Australian units and the 9th United States Army Air Forces TWC Headquarters. Today, the control tower has been renovated for the offices of a storage company, the huge hangars being the storage facilities. The land is now known as Normanton Airfield.

The interim period from after the war to the storage company was when the rumours began to circulate of the place being haunted. Local children would have played there, and the curious and those looking for mementoes or something left behind would have frequented the site. Only the foolhardy would have gone up there at night. Tales of weird lights and the drone of Merlin engines heard on the wind would deter nocturnal visitors.

Shortly after the storage firm took the site, several reports were received of inexplicable happenings. Workers and drivers arriving claimed to see strange flashing lights up at the gaunt shell of the old control tower, usually around dusk and early on dark mornings. One driver arriving at the depot spoke of observing a solitary figure near the tower. It appeared as a man dressed in an Irvin type sheepskin jacket with a flying helmet. The driver watched the silent figure slowly fade.

A party of ghost hunters from Nottingham learned of the case and approached the company with a proposal to evaluate the claims. Permission was given for them to spend a night in the control tower. They would arrange periods of watch and conduct the observation in a scientific manner. Unfortunately they saw no lights or apparition but noted a definable presence about the place. They cut short their time there as the intense cold temperature of the night became intolerable.

In 1981 another sighting came to light. A local man was indulging in his passion of visiting old military airfields. He had moved away from the old hangars and was approaching one of the runways when all of a sudden a figure appeared from nowhere. The man stopped in his tracks. The figure, who looked like a wartime flyer, began to move then just vanished. Then voices and laughter filled the air. The man was quite badly shaken up by these happenings.

A few months later another sighting was reported. This time it was the same figure standing on the control tower balcony looking out over the overgrown runway. Senior Aircraftsman (Retired), Robert Waldram, who had been based at RAF Conningsby and Wittering, explained that several active air force bases have their ghosts. The matter tends to be played down but of course creeps into idle conversation periodically. He had heard of airmen paying casual visits to old airfields claiming to have had strange experiences. We may conclude that these phantoms of the airfields linger or return in visitation as the camaraderie that many would have shared or the plain fact that after a particularly hazardous mission the familiar sight of the airfield would have been a blessed relief, a comfort. I would offer the conjecture that these silent phantoms are in their own dimension of time, totally unaware of the present. For them it is all there: the 'crates', the adrenaline, the noise, excitement and in many cases the pure dread. For us though, there is just the wind blowing across a barren field and quiet empty buildings.

Railway ghosts

Many of us will still remember the old steam trains, the mighty engines gleaming and with their own names. At one time in Leicester there was three large railway stations, not only London Road but also at Great Central and Belgrave Road. There were stations everywhere and one could travel anywhere. In comparison to today these trains were a lot slower but at least affordable and they ran to time. Even today the old steam trains have a huge following. Countless books, VHS video tapes and DVDs are available, shelves in toy shops groan under the weight of model engines, carriages and rolling stock with train sets still high on Santa's list. Of course the various steam preservation trusts with the sterling efforts of the volunteers and their boundless enthusiasm have provide an opportunity to relive the past. No wonder then that there may be other reminders of this bygone age. A lady from Thorpe Satchville would regularly take an evening walk with her dog. Part of the route included a section of cutting where the old line used to be. On one such excursion in 1989, the lady felt there to be something unusual, a mild feeling of unease. Then, in the distance she made out a train standing still. The train had three carriages and appeared quite old. The engine had a tall smokestack, not unlike Stephenson's *Rocket*. There were also people standing around. The men wore tailcoats and some had top hats. The women wore fine crinoline and some held parasols. The lady could just hear them chatting and she felt they were either unaware of her presence or simply could not see her. Her dog seemed unaffected by the spectacle. She watched for around five minutes then observed everything slowly fade away.

The lady was not intimidated by the experience but obviously amazed. She would no doubt have wished someone else to be with her to have seen it also. She did indeed speak of the incident and learned that the area had a weird reputation but was told of one episode whereby a man riding a pony along the same stretch was thrown as the animal suddenly reared up as if spooked by something.

The lady and her dog returned to the scene many times after but never saw the vision again. She did, however, feel a little unsettled at times though and as a result stopped walking by the old railway.

* * * *

An old stretch of railway between Higham on the Hill and Wykin near Hinckley is said to be haunted by a long-past tragedy. Again, this story involves a lady walking her dog The lady who was in her advancing years and quite deaf would regularly walk her dog, Spot, then let him off the lead in the fields adjacent to the railway line. One day in 1885 tragedy struck, Spot was off his lead in the field when he suddenly ran away. The distraught lady called after him but he was away then out of sight. The lady followed his path constantly calling for him. She then decided to see if he was on the railway. She clambered through a gap in the hedge and walked along the line calling 'Spot!'. Of course with her being deaf and shouting herself she was totally unaware of the coal train bearing down on her. The engine driver ferociously pulled the chain to release the steam valve for the whistle and apply the brakes but it was too late, she was killed instantly. Sometime after the accident stories began to circulate of a distant call, a woman's voice shouting 'Spot!'. It must be the ghost of the hapless dog walker unable to rest as she still searches for her elusive hound. This tradition has been strengthened in recent years as the barking of an unseen dog has been reported to answer the mysterious shouts.

* * * *

The Great Central Railway is well known to steam enthusiasts. It runs steam trains from Birstall to Loughborough with stations at Rothley and Quorn. Rothley station is quite a busy place for visitors. Not only may one admire the many period artefacts and see the trains but there is also a miniature working railway, a steam buff's paradise!

By night it changes. In 1983, a young man from Mountsorrel went into Leicester to a party at a house in Mowmacre Hill. The party went on quite late and among the few sober individuals there, only had a few cars and no one was going anywhere near Mountsorrel. It was a pleasant night, so he decided to walk home. He then remembered the railway line, a straight run better than the road. Birstall station was nearby, he could then walk the line to Rothley then onto home from there.

If the lad was the worse for drink, the trek would have indeed sobered him up, anyone who has walked a fair distance along a railway line will know that, this was a distance of two miles in almost total darkness.

Eventually the goods sheds came into view, then the rolling stock and the little station. He was unfamiliar with the station but assumed there was a way out onto the road up a flight of stairs at the bridge end of the platform. He had just got onto the platform when he noticed a figure moving about. The young man stopped and peered across. The figure looked like a man in some kind of uniform with a peaked cap like a stationmaster. The figure showed the mannerisms of awaiting a train. The young man then felt an awful feeling that turned to blind terror. He backed off and ran across the sidings then climbed over a fence to get away.

He was so affected by the encounter that he felt compelled to visit the station and talk to someone. A week later he duly did. He found a man dressed very similar to the figure on the platform. This was Stuart Bailey, the Rothley stationmaster. The young man explained everything. Mr Bailey told him that trains did not run late at night but then added that there were rumours of the station being haunted. Apparently there had been reports of mysterious figures in Victorian and Edwardian dress.

As well as hosting special events with a theme, the steam trust put on a bonfire and fireworks display on every 5th November. Not only is this a good way of publicising the railway but also helped with funds for the trust. As well as this, it is a useful method of disposing of any timber and other debris.

One year a rubbish skip was hired as with all large bonfires there is plenty of rubbish to dispose of. The evening before, one of the senior members of staff arrived at the deserted station to see that the skip had been delivered. He could not see it anywhere in the large car park so assumed it would be behind the old goods shed. Some distance along the track bed, a person passed him. At this time the track bed was often used by locals so it was not a trespasser. However, he had the urge to turn and look back at the person, but he or she had gone, vanished into thin air. In 2005, a study by a team of mediums from Melton Mowbray established many ghosts around the station.

Not far from Rothley station there used to be a small bridge over an access track for a farm near Swithland Lane. In the 1930s this was used on a regular basis for the farmer to get to his poultry and pig pens. During the winter months the track would become very boggy and sometimes flooded so the farmer would often cut across the track. This of course was very foolhardy as at this time the route was a busy main line and the signalman at the nearby Swithland signal box had had stern words with him on more than one occasion. The farmer worked it so his perambulations were before dawn or after dusk so he would not be seen. Eventually his luck ran out and he was struck and killed by a passing train. For many years after the signalman and other railwaymen would glimpse the ghostly farmer quickly running across the track.

* * * *

Although many of the old stations have long gone there is still evidence of their existence. Many a small town or village will have a row of cottages and most often a pub called The Midland or The Railway. In many cases there will be dark blue brick remains of a bridge nearby. During the age of steam, every boy's dream was to be an engine driver. Not all of them got their dream but many left school and got a job on the railway. Many would remain for their entire working lives. Those with a passion to travel would be firemen, guards, ticket collectors or work in the buffet car. The ambitious would work their way up to station master while others were content as porters, signalmen, tracklayers or wheeltappers. The latter was a very responsible job requiring a very keen ear and hefty biceps. Every wheel would be 'tapped' with a heavy hammer test the clarity of the ringing sound; should the report be dull, metal fatigue had set in.

As to who or what task the phantom railwayman of South Wigston had is anyone's guess. The mysterious figure haunts the vicinity of Wigston sidings, the area at the rear of several presently derelict factories on Canal Street up to Crow Mill Bridge on Countesthorpe Road. There used to be a row of cottages in the area where the factories now stand. There are still some on Pullman Road across the sidings, they are called Midland Cottages. It is thought the phantom may be a railwayman who lived in one of the cottages near Canal Street was crushed and killed. There have been all too many nasty accidents and fatalities so this is quite feasible. Several factory workers have claimed to have seen the dark figure trudging past the factory yards, most often around a winter's dusk. Some say he carries a lantern. He dresses in a navy uniform with a peaked cap suggestive of around the 1940–50s.

Probably the most recent account dates to 1991. Samantha Lambpet, then aged 15, attended Guthlaxton College on Station Road. One summer lunchtime, Samantha and four friends decided to visit a 'spooky building' over on the old sidings to play with an Ouija board as a laugh. They crossed the busy road then past the 1851 pub then down onto the waste ground. The girls entered the dank chill with the familiar smell of such places. They found a clear patch on the litter strewn floor to set up the Ouija board. Suddenly a man dressed in a blue uniform and wearing a peaked cap entered the building. He was tall with a thick moustache. He glanced over at the dumbstruck girls then strode across the building then exited at the far end. The giggling girls then hastily packed up and ran out. The man was nowhere to be seen.

While furnishing me with this account, Samantha admitted that at the time she had no knowledge of any phantom railwayman or that the man passing through might have been a ghost. To her and the others it was just a railway official. After hearing of the ghost in 1999 she was left to ponder on the matter. If it was a railway worker he seemed quite well dressed and the nearest railway station at South Wigston was quite a distance and was usually unmanned. Presumably a track worker at this time would have had a fluorescent orange coat or tabard. Why did he not speak or at least ask the girls to leave and why would want to wander the old sidings and the old building? Yet another intriguing mystery.

The Greyhound, Lutterworth

Old coaching inns have long held a tradition for having a ghostly presence or two. Like all long standing alehouses there will have been much festivity, drama and perhaps tragedy. Some of these events may be absorbed into the very fabric of the building creating a unique atmosphere.

The Greyhound in Lutterworth appears deceptively small when viewed from the road. It is only when one enters by the quaint and pleasant courtyard does one discover that it is quite a sizeable property, a roomy lounge area with the dining room and kitchens then a comfortable olde worlde bar. There are many guest rooms with narrow, winding corridors and a large function room in the basement.

Some have claimed that at times there is a tangible 'something' about the place, stronger than just an atmosphere. Interestingly this 'something' is not confined to one particular area and has been experienced in a number of locations. Charlotte, the daughter of owner, Robert Eggleston, is fairly sceptical but admits that some of the rooms occasionally exude an uncanny atmosphere. She has been told of residents in some rooms waking in the early hours to see a shadowy figure standing stock still at the foot of the bed. In 1998 one guest claimed to have observed a wretched-looking man hanging from the ceiling!

One or two of the cleaning staff are convinced the hotel is haunted. Several have heard their names being whispered by a disembodied voice. Mr Eggleston has not experienced anything himself and is totally sceptical of the suggestion of ghosts. Chef, Mike Lenton, however, does believe in the possibility of their existence after an incident that occurred late one evening in 2004. After a very busy evening, everyone had at last gone. He began locking up. Entering the lounge he glimpsed a young girl disappearing into the corridor towards the kitchens. Mike stopped dead in his tracks then hastily walked to the corridor. He opened a fire door to see where she had got to and was surprised to find no one there at all. He had certainly not imagined it and had noted she was wearing a white dress and had long brown hair.

In early March 2005, two friends of mine who live in Lutterworth, Bill and Susan Renton, were sitting chatting in the bar at the Greyhound. The subject of ghosts somehow crept into the conversation. Jane, the bar manager piped up that there was supposed to be a ghost at the

The beautiful courtyard at the Greyhound Inn, Lutterworth.

Greyhound. Then, a young lady who was at the bar buying a round of drinks became involved in the debate. She happened to be a journalist and showed much interest in doing a feature for the *Lutterworth Mail.* Susan then mentioned that she knew a ghost hunter which interested the journalist, Lindsay, even further. Susan passed on my contact details. A few days later, Lindsay telephoned and a date set for the visit.

On a dark and cold Saturday 17 March I arrived in Lutterworth to meet freelance photographer Andrew Carpenter at 6.30 p.m. for the obligatory photo shoot. Lindsay would come over around 9 p.m.. As the inn was very busy Andrew suggested going to a nearby churchyard for the photo shoot. I have lost count of the number of times I've had my picture taken in eerie church porches or sinister churchyards. I had to lean over a lichen covered tombstone brandishing a video camera; I making sure my light brown suede jacket did not get covered in green lichen. After fifteen or so exposures, Andrew was happy. He was now free to enjoy his Saturday night. I returned to the Greyhound to meet Bill and Susan, who had kindly offered to put me up for the night at their palatial residence, Rex Lodge, on the outskirts of Lutterworth. We then went for a meal at a small pub, the Unicorn. The meal is excellent; I am somewhat unadventurous and opted for my usual delight, humble steak and chips. I offered to pay for the meals but Bill insists. I can buy at least another round of drinks.

We arrived back at the Greyhound just after 9 p.m.. Susan spotted Lindsay who was with her sister. Bill went to the bar. We found a quiet corner in the lounge. Lindsay lost no time in telling me what she had gleaned. There are rumours that a murder took place here but as to the victim or when remains unconfirmed. Interestingly there is an idea that a small girl who lived in a cottage adjacent to the inn tragically fell down a deep well. I had inspected a well in the courtyard that must have been some forty feet deep. Lindsay told me that it was another well outside near the kitchens. This was the vicinity where Mike the chef saw the mysterious young girl.

Bill returned with the drinks and further cheerful introductions were made. The area was quite low lit and Bill was not wearing his spectacles. He said to Lindsay, 'Hello, I'm Bill, is this your daughter?' 'No, it's my older sister'. I broke the uncomfortable silence by suggesting a visit to at least one of the bedrooms where claims of activity had occurred. Jane was consulted and unfortunately the rooms in question were all taken. It was suggested we visit the function room in the basement and the vicinity around the kitchens and little rear yard.

I then explained to Lindsay the likelihood of actually experiencing anything would be most unlikely. Such happenings are very rare indeed and occur spontaneously. All we could do was to explore the areas quietly and calmly. Lindsay asked if I had brought along any gadgets. I had brought a video camera with infrared refinements, a thermocouple and an electrometer, the latter being a handheld device for registering any abnormal build-up of electrons or photons. Electrons are negatively charged atomic particles. Some apparitions have a source of light and affect artificial light; photons are basically a particle of light, a quantum measurement. My electrometer was built by Dr Rash Patel of Leicester University Engineering Department. It is a grey plastic box with a green panel meter, a switch for calibration, a large telescopic aerial and a red LED light. As an additional refinement Dr Patel put in a low back-light on the panel meter for use in darkness.

Lindsay, her sister and I embarked on our tour. First we went down the dark passage where the child was seen then out into a small yard. A huge well, very deep immediately got my attention. It has a fairly low surrounding wall and quite possibly a child could overbalance while peering down the wet gloomy hole. It would be a truly horrific end. Thick steel mesh is now in place over the chasm. We then entered a small outhouse which was in use as a storage area. I had enlisted Lindsay to operate the video camera while I tried a few sweeps with the electrometer; nothing worthy of interest seemed evident. No variations in temperature were found either. In the basement area we agreed that there was something atmospheric but difficult to pin down. I strolled over to the other side of the room and left the electrometer on a table then returned. One wall is a huge mirror and it was surreal to catch our own images in peripheral vision in the almost complete darkness. I decided to try a bit of evocation. I simply pulled a name out of a hat, 'Mary, if you're around please tap once.' We stood in silence, there was no response. But, the LED on the electrometer began to intensify. Very slightly, then faded out. There have been instances where apparatus has signalled some definite change for several minutes during evocation attempts. Unfortunately not tonight. After twenty minutes we all agreed to return to the lounge. At least Lindsay has had an idea of the rudiments of a typical ghost hunt, be it only in brief.

Jane came over and asked how it went. Then yet more drinks were ordered. Lindsay and her sister departed then we all had a long relaxing conversation in the now-closed inn. We left around 12.30 a.m.. No ghosts were seen or heard but is of no consequence as it was an interesting evening in a lovely old inn.

Bradgate

A large proportion of Leicestershire people will be familiar with the magnificent Bradgate Park. A huge oasis of tranquillity where one may idly wander the paths and crags where little has changed for many centuries. A place where most are glad to shed the rigours of modern life, there are a few though who deem it necessary to have a mobile telephone to their ear in case they lose touch with civilisation.

Bradgate was one of several parks surrounding Charnwood Forest; wild stretches of wooded country with rough tracks thought to have been made before the Romans – maybe even by Druids. Hunt's Hill with its wide tracks are believed to have been formed by many horses as the hill was a meeting point of great antiquity.

No excursion to Bradgate Park would be complete without visiting the ruin of Bradgate House. Built by Sir Thomas Grey, the Marquis of Dorset, the house took over ten years to build. Sadly Sir Thomas had perished before its completion in 1501. Bricks were quite a new idea and they were made at the southern end of what is now Cropston reservoir where there was evidence of a clay pit at the early part of the last century. The stonework and floor tiles are believed to have come from Ulverscroft Priory. The house was indeed a sizeable residence, some two hundred feet from east to west. At each corner an octagonal tower stood, two of which exist in a reasonable condition today.

The tower on the right if viewing the ruins from the wide path is locally known as 'Lady Jane's Tower'. Reputedly, the young Lady Jane Grey would retreat here to gaze over the park if in deep thought or troubled. She became an unwilling pawn in the Tudor power struggles becoming Queen for just nine days. She was executed at the Tower of London on 13 February 1553.

The Greys eventually retired to Staffordshire and the house was simply left to the harsh elements. As the building slowly deteriorated locals with carts would come and take bricks, slates and whatever other useful materials they could find. By the early seventeenth century this once-grand residence was a very sorry sight indeed.

Hound and horse racing took place on a course over a mile long near Hunt's Hill. 'Old John', a folly, was used as a grandstand and lunching spot. There is still evidence of a stable building below the steep crags. Old John itself dominates the skyline and there is a popular idea that the folly came about as a result of a tragic accident. In 1786 at the coming of age of the fifth Earl's son, a large bonfire was built on the hill. An old miller, John was given the task of building the fire and watching over it. A large pole around which the fire was built fell and killed old John. When viewed from a certain angle the structure resembles an ale tankard. Perhaps the folly is a tribute to the rustic old character who loved his ale.

Twelve farms vanished beneath the dark waters of Cropston Reservoir when it was flooded in 1869. The huge body of water covering two hundred acres was stocked with fish, including trout. Additionally work was done creating a series of pools in the River Lyn in order for silt to settle before it reached the reservoir.

The 7th Earl of Stamford's niece, Katherine Duncombe, inherited the estate of Bradgate and several neighbouring parishes. She sold Bradgate Park to the successful shoe magnate, Charles Bennion, who later presented the park to the city and county of Leicester; and other benefactors added land to create the beautiful park we have today.

Bradgate Park attracts around one million visitors a year. For those who can live without their mobile phones and other gadgets they will be left with just the sweet sound of undisturbed nature. If one stays a little late, after dusk there are other sounds, the deer, peacocks and small nocturnal animals, and maybe even the sounds of excited voices and gaiety.

A small party of late visitors were sitting on the bench near the little bridge over the River Lyn. They heard the voices approaching and casually watched for the crowd to come into view along the path. But the crowd never appeared and the voices seemed to pass by then diminish. Ghosts or just a strong breeze bringing distant voices from other late visitors?

It was not the breeze or imagination that caused the three sharp bangs, like a military drum being struck, that was heard by a party of late visitors passing the ruin one fresh April night in 1995. On their approach they saw the sudden exodus of all the deer and birds which they were certain had not left because of them. There was then a dreadful change in the atmosphere. It had become 'heavy' and someone mentioned a feeling as if something was going to happen. They all stopped and observed the silent silhouette of Bradgate House. Then another three sharp bangs got their full attention. With bated breath they awaited developments, expecting something else to occur but the oppressive atmosphere lifted. The deer slowly returned and the baffled group continued their journey.

Not only unexplained sounds but sights have also been claimed. A lady took her grandchildren to the park one weekday morning in spring, accompanied by her little and lively Scotch terrier. They were not alone in the park as there was a steady stream of visitors wandering around. When they reached the ruins she decided to casually stroll over to examine the remains and see if the notices advised when they were open to visitors. The grandchildren stayed near the circular cement drinking fountain. Almost as she arrived after the steep climb up the hill her dog began barking excitedly. She looked over to see a tall man approaching. He moved with long strides, he was very weather-beaten, long hair in a ponytail and he had a leather eye patch. The man, who the lady assumed was one of the rangers, wore a heavy brown coat and riding boots. As she was about to ask him about the ruins she felt odd as he was storming right up at the wall, he then passed through it and disappeared. The dog was now going crazy. As the lady told this account to me, she had no inclination he was a ghost until he stormed into the wall. Then this terrible shock set in.

In 1942, young Ray Belfield had his photograph taken by the little bridge in the Newtown Linford entrance to the park, one of several taken during this family outing. When they were developed there was a blurred but still definable image of a man wearing a dark habit like a monk, standing in the churchyard of the nearby All Saints church. Apparently he was not seen at the time the photograph was taken.

Of course the most well-known tradition here is the annual appearance of Lady Jane Grey. According to the legend, at midnight on Christmas Eve a coach leaves the old ruins then travels the short distance to All Saints Church. Lady Jane leaves the coach and the whole spectacle vanishes. Presumably someone has been a witness as in a mention in a 1926 edition of the *Leicester Illustrated Chronicle* she is described as 'dumpy'. There is another version that this occurs on New Year's Eve. I have yet to hear first hand of any sightings but a lady cycling through Newtown Linford at late afternoon on a Christmas Eve apparently heard a sound like several horses in close proximity. I have been informed that on Christmas Eve visitors do go in and stand by the main path in the hope of seeing the spectacle; they are likely to be disappointed. Perhaps they would be wiser to go up to higher ground or watch from the car park as the actual entrance for the Grey's was at the back of the house and would have journeyed along a route far from the comparatively recent main path.

There is alleged to be a large white phantom horse with red trappings seen galloping in the park. There are certainly no horses presently grazing here but of course there had been for centuries so this may be feasible.

Two late visitors, Dave Flanagan and his son Peter, claim to have seen a mysterious figure moving around erratically carrying some kind of lantern up near the wooded spinneys. On another occasion during August they watched a young female dressed oddly for the time of year, in a thick woollen shawl and hood; she came close to the pair and seemed totally unaware of them.

A person claiming to be clairvoyant stated that parts of the park were quite active with past events. With its unspoilt and unchanged scenario creating a relaxed atmosphere it would be quite feasible for individuals of a sensitive nature to be even more receptive and thus more likely to see and hear things.

One fine sunny morning in July 1969, a relief milkman was driving an electric milk float. He had just left the village of Cropston heading towards Swithland when in the distance he saw a carriage pulled by two horses. It seemed to come across the road from right to left then out of sight. When the milkman shortly arrived at the point where the carriage vanished it was clear to him the matter was odd indeed. All that was to his left was the reservoir. The wall was undamaged and there were no large ripples or anything else to suggest the thing had existed.

The park trust play down any idea of ghosts. The rangers are particularly uncomfortable with the idea. However, one member of staff did speak out to a friend of mine regarding one baffling incident. Apparently two members of staff were in the old boathouse next to the reservoir when a column of grey mist rapidly moved past them and vanished; it was described as 'not of this world.'

Strange clusters of dancing lights, a little like handheld sparklers, have been observed both static and moving along at speed. Also a greyish illuminated mist was seen traversing the outer west wall of the ruins. A very odd effect was seen in the vicinity of where the land begins to flatten out after 'Little Matlock', the very steep cliffs as one enters the park from Newtown Linford. The effect, that was firstly assumed as a small patch of water, was at first scoffed at. Sometimes in dark conditions such puddles appear as a lightish shape. Then, this lightish shape begins to change, it seemed to become like two sheets of greyish paper that entwine before fading from sight.

Of course the park after dusk can be a foreboding place, when an innocent fallow deer caught in peripheral vision is a convincing 'apparition', and the various birds around the reservoir can create some very eerie screams, and a vixen will indeed send a shiver up the spine with its bloodcurdling groans.

On the evening of 1 January 1996 I received a telephone call from a friend, Angela. She and her daughter, Jessica had gone to Bradgate and had stayed well after dusk in the hope of experiencing the phantom coach of Lady Jane Grey. It was a damp, misty evening and visibility was very limited. This later became worse when heavy fog set in. They found their way onto the main path after deciding to give up the idea and return to Newtown Linford. Then, Angela thought she saw a solitary figure standing to their right in the low bracken. Visibility was around thirty yards and the figure was only just in view. Jessica saw something so they assumed he was one of the rangers, he had a crew-cut and some sort of jerkin type garment. They quickly passed looking straight ahead. Then panic set in as Angela sensed the figure was coming after them. They both somehow got separated in their haste to get away and blind panic took over. Thankfully they did find each other and leave the park. Then they telephoned me.

I later met them to go over the incident in finer detail. It could not be ruled out that the figure could merely have been, as thought, a ranger or even another late visitor, perhaps one of several who were further into the fog. Fog of course creates a weird acoustic effect which may make one feel unsettled. The pair's prior knowledge may well have built up a subconscious image of a ghostly vision and expectation, as they had gone there for the sole purpose of experiencing a paranormal effect.

But having said that, I was not there, and they maintained adamantly of encountering something unearthly that January evening.

Haunted pubs

On the whole, pub ghosts are a cheery bunch. Of the ten thousand or so recorded haunts in England, a major percentage seems to be pubs. Most of the phantoms are considered as part of the furniture and a few have 'pet names' such as 'Fred'. Some pubs will have a chair reserved or a polished tankard kept for 'Old George' who probably spent most of his waking life in his favourite corner seeking solace from his moaning spouse. Unsurprising then that he may continue to 'pop in' now and again. I am happy to confirm that Leicestershire has its fair share of haunted pubs.

The Woodsman's Stroke in Rothley has a ghost known as Gregory. His identity is unknown but one theory is that he originates from when part of the property was a funeral parlour. Another suggestion is that Gregory was a man who resided at the pub until the First World War, when he enlisted and was killed in action.

Apparently he tends to inhabit the older parts of the place that date back to the twelfth century so perhaps his origins are in the distant past.

For most of the time Gregory stays aloof but on odd occasions he causes shelves to vibrate wildly, throws stools about and slams doors. The regulars are well aware of him and some have felt his tangible presence. Appearances are very rare but he appears as a quite large, shadowy figure.

I interviewed the young man who ran the pub on a pleasant August evening in 1999 – we did it alfresco fashion in the lovely garden over a beer or six. He had not experienced anything himself in the five years as licensee but spoke of the previous hosts, John and Beryl, who had both heard and seen Gregory.

One morning, Beryl was walking through the lounge when she saw a tall, dark man standing in the doorway. The pub was not open so Beryl explained that he was too early, then, the man vanished in a flash. A few months later, Beryl was awoken in the night by having her shoulder shaken vigorously. She peered into the gloom to see what John wanted but he was fast asleep. A handprint appeared on one of the small window panes that would re-appear whenever wiped. Experts from Nottingham University studied it and could put forward no satisfactory explanation.

* * * *

'Why haven't you served that chap sitting at the bar?', asked Linda, landlady of the Shakespeare Inn, Braunstone, one evening in 1999. The befuddled barman had just left the bar, there was no one there.

It was the first day of June, nearly 8 p.m.. The pub has three separate bars. To aid service a closed circuit television unit was installed. Linda noticed a man sitting at the counter on a high stool, there was no drink before him so naturally she was confused as to why he had been ignored. 'Chap, what chap, there's no one there'. So who was the man who appeared on the CCTV?

A few weeks later, a public relations company contacted me regarding the matter. The tape was handed onto my colleague and photographic expert, Wally Wilford, for analysis. There had been one or two peculiar incidents at the pub, a freezer unit had blown up, the glass washing machine frequently went haywire and furniture would mysteriously move of its own volition. One early morning cleaning lady complained of having a door violently slam in the toilets.

Linda could only assume the mystery figure to be a former regular but she did not recognise him. The image itself was somewhat blurred but depicted a man of middle age with an open necked shirt and a casual sports jacket, he could be from the 60s to the 90s.

Wally's eventual hypothesis was that the short footage indeed showed a man who appeared to be sitting at the counter. It was genuine enough but as to whether it was a ghost was open to opinion.

* * * *

Straying out of Leicestershire to the far side of Rutland, the Bluebell Inn in Belmesthorpe was built on the site of an ancient monastery which may explain the periodical aroma of incense pervading the pub in the night. It might also explain the shuffling monk with a hunched back reputedly haunting the pub and, in particular, outside near where an old well existed. He was seen by one former landlady quite often when she was locking up at night

There may be other phantoms however. Recently the landlord, a few regulars and a party of ghost hunters spent a night seeing what was abroad. During the night a tripod-mounted video camera was tampered with, there was a short appearance of a man in military uniform and someone complained of having something paw his leg, like a small animal. It was later discovered a phantom cat haunts the lounge!

* * * *

The Talbot Inn on Thurcaston Road in Belgrave boasts not one but five phantoms! They are a colourful collection indeed. Only one of them, however, has a nickname: 'Hairy Mary'. She is so named because of her wild tresses. She died on the premises in childbirth many years ago.

In the comfortable lounge, near the fireplace, some have felt a mild presence, nothing nasty though. Perhaps this is the ghostly small boy that was seen early one evening by a barmaid. She wondered where he had come from so she decided to go and ask him. She left the bar and walked to the lad who was sitting on a stool and giving a cheerful grin, when she got close the boy just vanished.

The Talbot Inn, Belgrave.

The pub itself is quite old and at one time was a coaching inn. It is claimed that some of Leicester's miscreants were brought here for a last meal then taken to the gallows at Red Hill for execution. Some were returned to a small mortuary for medical science experiments. The mortuary stood in what is now the pub car park. This might explain an incident several years ago. A former landlady was out gardening near the car park. Something distracted her attention, a chilly breeze, then a notable temperature drop. She then became completely unsettled and swiftly looked behind to see a small man with a hazy aura standing totally still. While she was trying to take in the vision, it slowly faded. The landlady was very shaken by the experience.

A mysterious image of a badly disfigured man has been seen peering into one of the pub windows from outside. Ghost hunter Robert Hincks discovered that a man was injured by a falling roof slate nearby and wonders if this is a psychic reflection.

Possibly the most interesting phantom is the fellow who emerges in the bar near where the pool table is situated. He has a cape raincoat which he lifts up in order to obtain a small leather purse, he then peers in and digs out a couple of pennies. Satisfied, he then proceeds through the wall and vanishes.

The present hosts, Robert and Sharon, have been there since 2000 and have enjoyed a ghost-free tenure. They are both sceptical of ghosts but perhaps one day...

* * * *

The waterside Hope and Anchor pub in Syston has an amiable if slightly fruity phantom known as Benjy. Rarely seen but often sensed, the chap goes along with the usual routine of banging doors and such like. He is thought to have become active after a partition wall was demolished revealing a staircase.

In 1996 I spoke to the licensee, John Man. Personally he had not met Benjy but felt accepted the ghost as part of the furniture of the seventeenth century inn. His wife and son though had heard whistling sounds and strange scratching noises in the dead of night.

On the whole Benjy is considered an integral part of the pub, not really a problem at all. The only known sighting was on a summer evening, when several regulars observed a hazy, transparent figure for just a few seconds. Some of the barmaids are a little wary however, as he has been known to pinch their behinds!

* * * *

No one relishes change, not even ghosts it seems. Many a phantom will be satisfied with its lot and have no reason to rattle its chains. In the summer of 2004 at the Red Lion in Great Bowden a noisy disturbance caused quite considerable mayhem.

The licensee had gone on holiday abroad with his family. Relief manager Gordon Insley would run the pub and live in during this period. Always a trying job, running someone else's pub, worried the regulars will moan about the beer. No one likes change. Anyway, Gordon soon settled in and built up a cheery rapport with the customers and staff, everything was fine, until one night.

Speaking from bitter experience (no pun intended), pub life is not exactly 9 to 5 and it is not uncommon to stay up quite late in order to 'wind down' after a busy evening session. Such was the case after Gordon had helped clean up and seen the staff off after the obligatory 'late one'. He went upstairs and decided to write a couple of emails on the computer in the little office.

It was deathly silent apart from the clicking of the keys. It was just after 2 a.m. when Gordon heard the sound of someone banging about in the cellar. He stopped what he was doing and listened. All was quiet, and then he heard the sound of someone coming up the stairs. Someone had broken in, burglars. Gordon quickly locked himself in then telephoned 999. While explaining to the operator a series of bleeping sounds and clicks caused communication problems, then, most oddly breathing sounds. The operator asked if he was pressing buttons or if there was a second person on another phone. Gordon explained that he was alone. The operator then instructed Gordon to remain in the office until the police arrived.

Shortly the police turned up en-masse sealing off each end of Main Street. With trepidation, Gordon left the office then cautiously went downstairs into the dark pub, he then opened the doors to the several police officers. After a thorough search and investigation it was found there was no evidence of anyone breaking in or signs of an intruder in the building. After the police departed, the understandably shattered Mr Insley stayed up for the remainder of the night.

The rest of his relief period was untroubled. He did of course mention the incident to the staff and some of the locals. There were rumours of a ghostly presence but little else. The pub itself was formed from two cottages in 1906.

I was later consulted on the incident and after consideration I could only suggest that it appeared as a classic case of psychic disturbance brought on by a change to the normal culture.

* * * *

The ghost of an old Irish navvy is believed to haunt the Wheel and Compass at Weston by Welland, just over the Northamptonshire border near Market Harborough. The ghosts reputedly has an odd quirk for turning water on. This most often occurs during the night but sometimes it just happens randomly. Other phenomena includes a cold patch moving around the kitchen, the sound of feet shuffling around at night, bottles of beer exploding, the electric grill switching itself on, and sweet perfume smells in the lounge.

Some years ago structural work was undertaken, including an entire new floor in the kitchen. A gravestone with Gaelic writing was discovered among the rubble; the stone was broken up and taken away with the rest of the debris. It is thought the navvy died here. Some think he was murdered and buried somewhere nearby. The idea seems to be that the building work and removal of the little memorial stone has disturbed his rest. Perhaps if deeper digging had taken place his bones would have turned up.

* * * *

As we have seen, structural work seems to unleash supernatural upheaval. This could be the case at the Three Horseshoes' at Stoke Golding. The work undertaken in the early 1970s included sealing up an ancient well.

In the early part of the twentieth century a group of Romany gypsies made camp on the edge of the village. The women would go around selling their wares such as lace and lucky heather. The heather was not very lucky for one young girl, Esmeralda. She went to the pub; it was closed so she wandered around the rear to find the other way in. Unknown to her, there was a deep well. Earlier the well had had been used and the large stone slab had been left aside. Esmeralda stumbled and fell in. The landlord and his wife heard her scream and rushed outside. Their attempts at rescue were in vain and the young girl drowned.

After the inquest her family took Esmeralda away for a gypsy funeral. A curse was put on the well but not the inn or the family.

Shortly after the well was sealed a strange feeling would permeate the pub now and again. Electrical oddities such as the lights dimming, periodical drops in temperature and staff complaining of being watched. On one occasion several stunned drinkers watched a young girl dressed in a long garment glide through the lounge then disappear.

There is nothing malevolent, if anything these presences seem to exude a feeling of tranquillity and good nature. Some have offered the idea that the sealing of the dangerous well has created the atmosphere and the spirit is pleased that no one else will endure her horrible passing.

* * * *

There are said to be a mixed bunch of lively phantoms at the Union Inn in Hinckley. In the cellar there is a finely-dressed highwayman seen regularly by the landlady. A ghostly 'regular' sits at his favourite table reading a book, and there is a mischievous child and a number of marching soldiers.

Apparently in the eighteenth century, wretches were executed in the town square and in some cases the bodies were placed in the cellars of the inn, where several skeletons have been discovered over the years.

* * * *

Of course many pub ghosts can exist for decades without disturbing anyone, then there will minor events that lead one to wonder. There will be a long succession of hosts having no ghostly problems then for some reason an inexplicable happening will lead to theories of a restless spirit acting up.

The Black Dog in London Road, Oadby, has retained that old pub charm that is something of a rarity these days. The licensees, Norman and Maureen Green, are the perfect hosts.

The pub was originally a coaching inn erected in the mid-seventeenth century and over the years has had more than thirty landlords. Some, like the clientele, were rather unsavoury characters: poachers, highwaymen and other reprobates. In 1897 the inn was bought by Lichfield Breweries then passed onto several others; it is now a Banks' house.

There is a large skittle alley that at one time was a stable then later a mortuary; this may have stirred the notion of a haunting. I was also told that a motorcyclist was killed when his machine crashed into the building in the 1950s. A colleague at Leicester University told me that there was rumoured to be some sort of ghostly presence at the pub so I arranged to visit one evening in March 2004. Asfordby-based psychic investigator Lynda Kinniburgh accompanied me.

Norman had only two anecdotes to relate. He explained that one evening a particular brand of beer suddenly stopped as he was pulling a pint. Norman was puzzled as the barrel could not have run out. Norman laboriously went down the cellar to see what had happened. He discovered the feeder tap had been turned off. Even more puzzled, Norman turned it back on and returned to the bar. The other incident occurred in the cellar. Norman was setting a kilderkin (eighteen gallon barrel) on the raised brick curb when the hosepipe used for rinsing the floors suddenly snaked about for a few seconds. A mystified Norman looked at the thing and inspected it but found nothing to cause the hose to behave so oddly.

Lynda suggested visiting the cellar so we all descended. After showing us the hosepipe Norman was told by Lynda that she had a faint impression of a young lad, only around five or six years old, who was residual in origin but attached to the place. She added that the child was from a long-past period but could not receive enough to offer even a century. She 'felt' his name began with the letter 'S'. The child liked Norman but was less than keen on me!

While back at the bar counter writing up notes another set of drinks were ordered so I asked Maureen if she had any cobs to soak the beer up. She had cheese and onion – tough work being a ghost hunter! I then told those present of the late, great parapsychologist, Andrew Green, who was employed by a large London brewery to help new licensees cope with the phantoms in the large number of haunted pubs the brewery owned. He would also advise and deal with any disturbances. What a job!

Maureen herself, although experiencing nothing herself, keeps an open mind on the prospect and mentioned that she had heard of a strange, darkish 'thing' that momentarily appeared in the lounge. She had been told by regulars of the motorcycle incident and wondered if this may be connected.

Norman took us over to the skittle alley. The old iron rings where horses were tethered remain and there was a definite musky odour to the place. Lynda picked up very little here but sensed a remnant of a stable hand, a young fellow, not actively haunting the place but a possible visitation.

We then went up to the top floor where three small rooms exist. The rooms were quite grim and appeared unused for many years. Lynda explained that the essence of the child in the cellar was evident here also. Back at the bar yet more drinks were ordered and an arrangement made to return later in the year with a larger party to conduct a study.

This took place on a hot evening in late August. Phil Rimmer was already at the bar. I presented Maureen with a box of chocolates and bought Norman a beer. The Loughborough contingent arrived shortly after; Louise presented me with a belated Christmas present, a small ornamental ghost complete with rattling chains! Then Lynda and her party arrived. I explained to Maureen that ghost hunters are a boozy lot and the takings would go up dramatically. After everyone had settled I nipped up to the top floor to leave an experiment running. The trifield meter was calibrated to bleep if a distortion field of electromagnetism formed and several articles were placed on the floor: a penny, a ball and a pen. Additionally I fixed a pencil to the foot of the door and some paper beneath. Should it move, I would know. A radio was placed and set to transmit so I could listen in downstairs.

Unfortunately this experiment was doomed as the radio batteries drained in less than five minutes. This seems to occur all too often on these studies.

Later on several of the party ventured upstairs, Louise felt a mild 'something' around the landing but no one else noted anything untoward. I had forgotten my torch and in the darkness I managed to nearly fall down the stairs. This brought much mirth to the others.

Lynda, Barrie and Dawn were in the skittle alley. Several tripod-mounted video cameras had been strategically positioned, devices to test for temperature and static fields were in place, and a circle of chairs arranged for a later psychic sitting. Lynda mentioned that one part of the skittle alley had abnormal surges of static electricity. Norman then locked it up and everyone relaxed in the lounge until closing time.

Those of a sensitive disposition established that the only area where activity seemed likely was the skittle alley so the entire party moved over to that building. Video cameras and the machines were activated as the first psychic circle sat. The lights were then switched off. Two names came up but felt to be of little value as they are mentioned on the pub's Web site. Towards the end of the second sitting, Steve jolted. Apparently something had struck his lower leg, some kind of missile. I was observing the circle with an image intensifier and saw no one playing any pranks so this was interesting. There were impressions of a wool merchant and someone connected with a tannery, but these were faint psychic impressions. The lights went on and we looked in vain for whatever had struck Steve.

The study had not confirmed or dismissed a haunting. Norman and Maureen are not perturbed by the prospect as the pub's ghosts, although occasionally mischievous, are a remnant of time and part of the atmosphere.

Ghosts of the road

Ghosts, it appears, like to get out and about and are to be found on quiet lanes and busy roads. The speeding motorist would be well advised, particularly on dark wet nights, to slow down in case such an apparition present itself.

One dark night in 1976, a motorist was driving to his home in Evington village. On Evington Road near the golf course the driver became aware of a shadow-like figure that walked off the grass verge into the road. The furious driver could not believe it, was this a deaf or blind person? As he was about to sound his car horn at the idiot, who was now in the middle of the road, he or she vanished. The perplexed driver pulled over and got out of his car. Despite a thorough search there was only himself on this dark and quiet spot.

* * * *

Again in the mid 1970s, a driver took pity on an old man shuffling along Gypsy Lane in Leicester late on a wet and windy night. He pulled up and offered a lift to the man who said nothing but stopped walking. Philip, the passenger got out and tipped his seat forward so he could clamber in the rear of the Ford Anglia. They then set off. The driver asked the old man where he was going but received no reply; he and his front seat passenger then both felt movement as the suspension eased. Philip turned around. The old man was no longer there. He could not have got out of a two-door, moving vehicle. Who or what was the old man?

* * * *

During a winter's dusk in the early 1990s an ambulance was travelling on the narrow, winding road that cuts from the A606 to the B674 between Oakham and Twyford. The vehicle had just passed through Burrough on the Hill. Then, as if from nowhere, appeared a small child dressed in a petticoat or thin nightgown. Both the driver and assistant saw the child. They passed by, then pulled over as they were concerned that a young child should be in the middle of nowhere on a cold evening. They left the ambulance and were surprised to find no child anywhere to be seen. Thankfully the vehicle was not in a hurry or the result could have been very dire indeed.

* * * *

In the mid-1990s there was an incident in which police, some with dogs, were dispatched to Gibbet Lane at Bilston. Apparently a motorist on his way to Atherstone had hit a large grey-haired man wearing a trench coat who had suddenly appeared in the road.

The driver was in shock as the man was not under the car but must have crawled to a ditch. Despite a full search of the area no one was found and there was no visible evidence of a collision on the vehicle. One officer felt quite disturbed by something and was unwilling to leave his patrol car.

This was not the only incident in which a character of this description has been seen. However, this may not be the only phantom in the area. The gibbet itself was erected to display the body of one John

Massey. Hated and feared, Massey was a heavy drinker and prone to fits of violent, drunken rages. In 1800, he attacked his second wife viciously then drowned her in the mill-race. Later, he dragged his ten-year-old step daughter to the pond and drowned her also, at least he thought he had.

She survived. Massey was hung at Red Hill gallows then left to rot on the gibbet near to the scene of his crime. A motorist observed two figures staring at the old gibbet post in 1979. One was a woman, the other was a girl aged around ten years old. Despite it being a fine, sunny day, the figures were both dripping wet.

* * * *

In 1994, Dave Burrows had just left the car park at Belvoir Castle in Leicestershire. He got onto the winding road to Knipton then spotted someone standing by the road. As he got nearer he realised the person, a man, was hovering above the ground. His lower legs were not in evidence. He appeared colourless, a dull grey. As Dave got almost level the figure simply moved into the path of car. Dave braked as the figure slowly vanished. Dave stopped and got out but there was no one anywhere.

* * * *

There have been at least two sightings of a mysterious figure on the A607 just past Waltham where the road forks for the village of Freeby. The first incident was on a cold, dark night in February 1989. A man and his wife were travelling towards Melton Mowbray. Shortly after passing the Freeby turn, a dark figure stepped into the road; the driver slowed down and as they passed the figure disappeared.

In October the following year just as dusk began to set in, a couple were going in the opposite direction towards Waltham. The lady who was the passenger watched a man running along the verge ahead and noted his very scruffy appearance. Idle curiosity then turned to mute terror as she realised her husband made no attempt to pull out to pass him. She shut her eyes and waited for the impact. There was no collision, she looked back but the man was gone. Her husband had not seen anyone at all. After an exchange of words the lady accepted she was either hallucinating or had seen a ghost.

The image or experience simply would not go away. The lady was adamant that what she had seen was real. She decided to try the local newspaper, the *Melton Times*, to find if the mystery might be solved. Her appeal yielded two interesting accounts. The first concerns a character locally known as 'Peppermint Billy'. He murdered his grandson and a toll keeper at Thorpe Arnold in 1856. The other possibility was a farm labourer who was run over by the Melton to Grantham stagecoach in 1886.

After careful consideration the lady opted for the latter suggestion as Thorpe Arnold is some two miles from where the incident took place. However, the unfortunate labourer met his untimely demise quite near to where she had seen the rustic-looking figure.

* * * *

A strange, menacing phantom lingers around Gibbet Hill crossroads where the Lutterworth Road crosses Watling Street. In the early 1900s a horse and trap was passing a gloomy hollow when the horse stopped in terror. The driver got down to see what was up when a tall, black, hooded figure stormed through a hedge then across the road where it stopped in front of a tree. It turned around to reveal a bone-white skeletal face.

In 1949, a party of ghost hunters decided to tour the area and struck lucky by parking at just the right spot. At around 11 p.m. a figure like a monk stormed across the road then vanished into thin air!

* * * *

As we have seen, these phantoms of the road tend to create a similar scenario. Our last phantom though is unusual in that it is not that of a person. On the A606 between Oakham and Melton there have been reports of a large, white shape streaking across the road. The thing simply appears then vanishes. An obviously terrifying experience and potentially dangerous on this hilly road.

The anomaly derives from a legend. A warrior chief had fought many battles atop his trusty white steed. His young son would also become a fine warrior. One day he placed the child on his horse but tragedy struck. The horse bolted and the child was killed. His father was not only grief stricken but furious. He found an axe and viciously hacked at the animal until it fell dead. The legend then states that over the following months as grief turned to remorse, the warrior became the vision. It is known as the 'White Horse of Leestone Hill'.

House calls

Cases of flare-ups of inexplicable happenings and disturbances in private residences are by no means uncommon. They nearly all follow a similar trend. I have been consulted on many such cases throughout England and of course Leicestershire. As a rule these cases are kept confidential but with the occupiers' co-operation I will relate a selection; some names have been changed for anonymity and house numbers altered to respect privacy.

One case actually involved three houses, numbers 78, 80 and 82 Red House Road, Glen Parva. The upheaval, which occurred over several weeks in 1986, became so unpleasant that one young girl at number 82 climbed out of a bedroom window and jumped; she broke several limbs as a result.

The worst of the activity seemed to be focussed at number 78, the Smiths' house. Towards the end of the turmoil an apparition of a man dressed in 'Cavalier-type garb' appeared in the living room. On one occasion a carriage clock stopped seconds before an appearance. Mrs Smith told me she could not grasp why these strange things happened and why it seemed to spread like a contagion. Bumps and bangs, an unsettling atmosphere and weird icy chills became common.

It later came to light that a coaching inn existed on the Lutterworth Road and the ground occupied by the three houses was once the stables. It was thought that something unpleasant occurred which caused a ghost to be created. Why it should suddenly flare-up for a few weeks in 1986 remains unresolved.

* * * *

The Kimble family were subjected to bizarre activity at their home in Portcullis Road, Leicester. Thickish fluid not unlike wallpaper paste would suddenly begin to seep from ceilings and walls. The viscous slime damaged some possessions and killed the pet goldfish. Sometimes visitors to the house would discover damp patches on their clothes and a lady found slime in her handbag. Very often this substance would dry with unnatural rapidity.

A clergyman who became involved glimpsed an apparition upstairs and explained that it was some sort of haunting.

Renowned ghost research Robin Furman managed to obtain a sample of the liquid which was hastily submitted to Leicester University. On analysis it was established that the liquid was animal urine but not a dog or cat. These happenings ran for three years from 1989 until 1992.

Whilst a member of the Society for Psychical Research I pressed the spontaneous cases committee for me to re-examine the case in 1993. The response was that the liquid had been analysed and had no paranormal origin. I begged to differ as the volume of the glutinous liquid and its unexplained source suggested that the case warranted thorough attention.

* * * *

An average semi-detached house in Frewin Street, Humberstone, was the scene of some dramatic phenomena that eventually drove the occupants out.

The Prices bought the house in March 1988. Everything seemed normal until June. Then doors would violently slam, loud footsteps were heard and a genuine feeling of unrest permeated the entire house.

Three clergymen were consulted and suggested crucifixes be placed around the house. One of the priests felt there was a spirit attached to the place.

Things then got worse. The banging intensified, then the ghost began to appear. A black undulating shape would form into a shadowy figure and strange circles of light and a fine mist would build up and move about the house.

As if this was not bad enough the disturbances then took on physical capabilities. Mr and Mrs Price endured having someone walking across their bed, the bed shaking, their hair pulled. Even the pet spaniel would yelp as if being molested. Eventually they had enough and left the house.

The house remained empty for quite a long time. I made an unsuccessful attempt at renting it for a month in order to experience the reported phenomena under controlled conditions.

It was discovered that the previous occupant, who lived alone, was placed in a bungalow as his legs were bad. He had lived at the house for fifty years and was very reluctant to leave. In June 1988, he lapsed into a coma and died at the end of July.

* * * *

Christine and Paul were busy getting their new home how they wanted it. Again, just an ordinary semi-detached house, in this case it was Willow Road in Shelthorpe, Loughborough. Everything was normal until work commenced on a small bedroom that would be a nursery room for their baby.

A tangible sensation of someone unseen was detected, there were unexplained footfalls on the landing, and doors opened and closed by themselves. Later the couple's bed lifted and jolted, and a drawer would continually open and slam shut. In November 1996 Christine telephoned me. We decided to arrange a short investigation and a date was set.

All sorts of experiments were tried, recording apparatus was left running on the landing and a video camera was positioned at various points. Random articles, (such as an old penny, plaques with letters on, a stiletto and a slate with chalk) were left in empty rooms should the phantom decide to 'inspect' them. Compasses, a barometer and thermometers were placed about the upstairs landing should there be a change in local atmosphere. Nights were spent in the house with nothing particularly unusual occurring, although I did get a fright when one of the two pet cats ran over my leg whilst I was dozing on the dark landing.

I asked Terry Hewitt of the Association for the Scientific Study of Anomalous Phenomena if he could bring a psychic medium over to the house. So the following Saturday evening Terry came along with not one but two clairvoyants.

Les, Julie, Terry, Christine and I all sat in the lounge over coffee before the tour of the house and rear garden. Firstly Terry went with the two clairvoyants then the pair went again without anyone present.

After a lengthy period, Les and Julie returned. They 'felt' that there were two presences in the house, a man with grey wavy hair, wearing dark clothes and smoking a pipe. He was very unhappy indeed and may well be responsible for the atmosphere and the disturbances. On the landing there was an impression of a scolded child locked in a cupboard; he emanated misery and desperation which could be easily picked up. The couple's child, Alex, may have been 'drawing' the spirits, acting as a psychic link between our dimension and the next.

Over the next few months things settled with just the odd minor anomaly. The most bizarre concerned a Christmas tree. This festive tree had a built-in effect so cheerful Christmas songs would play periodically. Late one night Christine got up as she heard the tones of *Jingle Bells*. Somewhat perplexed she stormed downstairs then into the lounge. The tree was brightly lit as well, but she was baffled as the electric plug was out of the socket!

Swithland

One of Leicestershire's most enduring ghost stories must indeed be that of the old Swithland Rectory. The terrible occurrences resulted in a haunting for many years and kept many villagers within earshot of the place safely indoors after dark.

The story begins in 1820. Swithland Rectory, like many others, was quite a large building. Many rectors enjoyed a quite salubrious living. Many had large families and would have employed staff to attend to various duties. There would have been a housemaid, a retainer, a governess, a gardener and general handyman. Some would live in while others would come over for an hour or two, these would live nearby.

The rectory at Swithland had a live in butler called Parker, a reliable, upright man for much of the time. Occasionally he would become a little bad tempered and on rare occasions have a foul temper.

The entire family went away for a holiday in Yorkshire leaving Parker alone in the rectory. Of course as soon as the place was his the stiff collar would have been discarded and he would have the run of the house instead of being confined to the kitchen chair or his small room. After a few days of being lord of the manor he felt one of his moods coming on. He loved a drink, he would not have dared to touch any of the whisky or brandy that he would decant but thought the well-stocked wine cellar would be worth a visit as no one would miss a bottle or two.

The day before the family were due to leave Yorkshire, the rector ordered his twenty-year-old daughter to return that day in order to prepare everything for the family's arrival. She was displeased at the prospect but agreed to do so. She travelled alone in a stagecoach eventually arriving at the Plough Inn at Loughborough then taking a smaller private carriage to the rectory, arriving late afternoon.

She pulled the brass bell chain and after a while Parker opened the door. His appearance and demeanour left a lot to be desired, he was

The Grey Lady of Swithland Church.

unkempt and appeared drunk. She would certainly bring this to her father's attention the next day. She felt it prudent to have as little to do with him as possible and ordered that he not disturb her as she was tired after all the travelling and would retire early. She felt very ill at ease and thought to lay on the bed still dressed in her grey brocade travelling dress. She lay there wishing Parker would retire for the night, as she could hear him shambling about downstairs. It was no good, she would stay awake all night if she had to, the man was like a lunatic and she must be on her guard. Despite her efforts she did eventually slip into a fitful doze.

She was abruptly awoken by the bang of the bedroom door being kicked open. In the failing light she saw Parker raging drunk; he just stood there swaying and muttering incoherently. Before she could scream, he was at her.

Further into the night Parker came round, he had passed out. He felt nauseous and had no idea where he was. With his head pounding he sat up. In the darkness he saw a truly horrific sight. His nausea rose as the horror dawned. He had murdered the rector's daughter, he had garrotted her. She was hanging by some cord around her neck and tied to one of the beams on the four poster bed.

With his stomach churning Parker realised he would hang for this. He stumbled out of the bedroom and went downstairs to the kitchen. He found a large carving knife then began hacking at his throat until he collapsed choking on his own blood. The family arrived later that day to discover the horrendous scene of murder and suicide.

In time, some of the villagers claimed to hear awful screams emanating from the rectory at night and there were sightings of Parker stumbling about hacking at his throat. Both victim and murderer were haunting the scene of this terrible event.

These hauntings continued until the rectory was pulled down after the First World War. There is a tradition that shortly after the demolition, a figure wearing a grey brocade dress and carrying a slab of stone from the ruined rectory glided off towards the church and was seen no more, a final appearance of the victim taking a physical reminder of the horror to a place of sanctuary.

Then there were claims of a ghost in the churchyard of St Leonard's. It was a young female wearing a grey dress. The phantom soon became locally known as 'The Grey Lady of Swithland'. The sightings tended to tie in with events at the church such as christenings, weddings and funerals and she appeared during a garden party. There were reports by locals passing of her wandering the churchyard on moonlit nights. These sightings then became scarce then ceased altogether.

I admit to spending more than a few late hours observing her haunting grounds. I never saw anything or experienced any of the sensations one may encounter in pursuit of these aloof spectres. A mixed blessing occurred in the early 1990s when a cluster of houses were built opposite the church. The positive angle being that a sighting might be reported by one of the residents, previously there was only the odd motorist passing by who would not notice the churchyard at all. The negative prospect was that this may hamper covert operations in that I or colleagues would be seen and assumed to be up to no good rather than merely watching the site.

On 31 October 2005, Halloween, the Griffin Inn in Swithland hosted an evening event called 'A Host of Ghosts'. The restaurant would be in darkness with just candlelit tables. Couples and groups would be told of ghostly tales over two forty-five minute sessions with a hearty meal during the interval – that great British sustenance 'bangers and mash'. I was booked as the teller. After a rather awful opening introduction the event got underway.

My first account was the Grey Lady. When I asked how many 'Swithlonians' were present only one couple piped up so most of the audience would be unfamiliar with the story. As I was finishing and mentioning the last appearance being decades ago I noted the local lady was almost gasping in anticipation so I asked, 'Any questions or comments?' 'It's been seen more recently than that,' said the lady. During the interval I 'mingled' and made a beeline for the Swithland couple. I was then furnished with a report of an interesting if short sighting. The lady was one of the bell ringers at St Leonard's church. During one evening practice in 1999 one of her fellow bell ringers tore up the steps and into the rope room, 'You'll never guess what I've just seen'. As he passed through the lychgate he saw a clear greyish form drift across the churchyard then abruptly vanish. So, the Grey Lady is still active perhaps.

The restaurant at the pub was once used as a mortuary and the landlord, David, told me of a reliable sighting of a darkish figure who was observed walking straight through what is now a fireplace. Also behind the restaurant is an ancient annexe to which a small staircase leads; one member of staff was given a firm shove down these by an unseen hand. Hallowe'en in a haunted restaurant!

The 'Host of Ghosts' was scheduled to finish at 9.30 p.m. but overran by about two hours. A small party stayed behind for an impromptu, in-depth discussion on ghosts. One thoughtful chap even bought me a drink which helped my vocal chords enormously.

As for the Grey Lady of Swithland, good news for me and fellow ghost enthusiasts but sad in that this tragic figure is still not at rest.

Grace Dieu Priory

About a half-mile west of the village of Thringstone stand the ruins of Grace Dieu Priory. Passing by at night, the motorist would not be the slightest aware of the fact, unless the ghost is abroad. There have been many sightings of a white figure here reported over eighty years.

The ruin itself stands in a field on the busy A512 road. A gate by the old railway bridge allows access to the field which periodically has livestock grazing; also I might add, some of the largest molehills I have ever seen!

In September 1926 a landau carrying eleven-year-old Hetty Wilson and her father was passing the ruin when the horse suddenly stopped

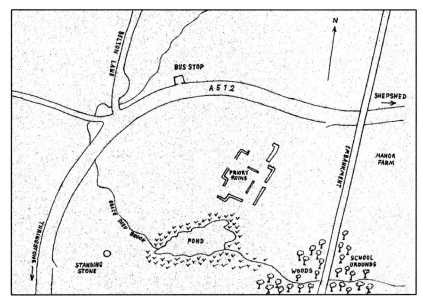

A sketch plan of the Grace Dieu Priory site.

in its tracks. The animal appeared traumatised and began trembling from head to foot. Then six white figures drifted across the road. Hetty was so scared she crouched down and hid her head. After a few seconds she peered up to see the apparitions, which had white robes, move into the ruin.

On a summer evening in 1934, several youngsters were playing cricket on Grace Dieu Park, situated behind the Bull's Head pub towards Thringstone. Young Tommy Allen caught sight of a white figure. He looked hard and realised it was a nun moving swiftly along near the footpath at the side of the park. Tommy shouted to his friend and brother who then saw it. They all began to follow and watched the figure enter the cattle creep under the railway embankment. The three boys then ran to the archway and through the tunnel, at the other end they discovered no one there.

Motorists have reported many strange encounters here. Around 1960 local historian Denis Baker was driving past the ruin when he noticed a woman ahead on the verge where the Belton Lane turn-off is situated. Then, to his horror the woman walked out in front of his car. He braked but was upon the woman. There was no impact and in his rear view mirror Denis then saw the woman carrying on across the road as if nothing had happened. She appeared quite solid and wore a long, pale garment.

In 1954 a bus driver stopped in order for a solitary woman to board. The woman was dressed in white and was clearly visible. The bus stopped but no one got on. The mystified conductor and driver actually left the vehicle to see where she could have gone, but they found nothing.

The figure was seen in the early 1980s by two separate motorcyclists. In one incident, the motorcyclist was a police constable. It was just after midnight, a warm August night. As he passed the old priory he noticed the air temperature plummet then a grey shrouded figure glided across the road in front of him. He was badly affected by the encounter.

A rare collective sighting took place in 1990. It was a dark spring night as the Lea family were travelling home from Loughborough. As the car approached the ruin, Mrs Lea exclaimed, 'Oh my God, what's that?' Standing next to the brick bus shelter was a vertical luminous shape. As the car passed the bus shelter everyone looked. The figure appeared impassive, it had no features or feet and was wrapped in a shroud-like dressing.

In 2002 a bus driver, Pete, was taking the last Coalville bus through Thringstone. He noticed a figure at the bus stop and slowed down, but the figure vanished. He mentioned it to the only passenger who said there had been many sightings of a solitary figure here.

The ghost or ghosts are not confined to the ruin or area of the bus stop. A whitish figure has been reported in the grounds of the nearby Grace Dieu Roman Catholic School. A similar looking figure was seen on Belton Lane and in the village.

The popular theory is that the ghost is attributed as Agnes Litherland, a prioress who, according to legend, met a violent death here. Tales of secret tunnels, drownings and being bricked up alive have fuelled the idea of her being the ghost. All so often fancy tales that become embellished 'explain' a ghost. In fact Agnes Litherland left the priory with fifteen other nuns and was totally unharmed.

The more plausible idea would be that the apparition reflects Roisia de Verdun, the foundress. She founded the priory in 1225 for Cistercian nuns. She died in 1247 and was buried in the chapel. During the Dissolution, her remains were discovered and re-interred at Belton church. In 1839 plans were made to have the remains restored to the priory but the rector of Belton church decided against the idea. As so many sightings have been near Belton Lane it has been suggested that the nun is trying to bring attention to her wish to have her remains restored.

Not only has the apparition been seen but has demonstrated physical phenomena on two occasions. In November 1997 several council workers were engaged in improvement works on the site. It was just before dusk as one man had just finished strimming. He looked around and saw a woman watching him intently then he received a sharp push in the back. He looked around but there was no one near, the woman had vanished. During a guided ghost walk on the Hallowe'en of 2003 there were three curious incidents. One of the guides was hit on the head by a stone, one of the visitors was pushed and everyone looked up at the scaffolding on the ruin to see who was walking along the plank staging but there was no one to be seen.

Two ambiguous photographs appeared in that year. On 26 March, two Canadians staying at Shepshed went over to Thringstone to have a meal at the Bull's Head. It was still light as they passed the ruin and over their meal they decided to visit the place afterwards as it looked 'spooky'. It was quite dark as they entered the field. They had a good look around the foreboding ruin and took several photographs on a new digital camera. They then returned to the pub as it had turned quite cold. On their return they perused the images more closely. One exposure showed a wispy effect. Supernormal photographs with hazy mists are often caused by cigarette smoke or exhaling breath vapourising. This however seemed of a more bizarre nature. The landlord and staff are well aware of the ghost and were highly impressed with the photograph. Later, the two Canadians sent the pub a large copy of the photograph.

The other photograph was taken on the night of 28 October, one of several obtained by a party of ghost hunters. There appears to be the upper torso of a man. There was no one around when the photograph was taken. A spiritualist medium, Jackie, showed little surprise upon viewing the image, she had 'observed' a soldier crossing the cycle path around the time the photograph was taken.

A third photograph that is most thought provoking was taken on 28 September 2005. A group attached to the Whitwick Historical Society visited the site for a twilight tour of the ruin. Also in attendance was John Dickinson of the Grace Dieu Archaeology Group. During the event, Anna, a friend of Mr Dickinson's eldest son, decided to take a photograph of the ruin with her mobile telephone camera. Only later was it discovered that a mysterious figure had been captured. The figure appeared to be under the large archway – a man dressed in black with a white cravat. It bore no resemblance to any of the visitors. Anna saw no one when she took the photograph. After it had been enlarged and a print taken, Mr Dickinson showed it to three mediums separately to see what the verdict might be. Although their impressions differed somewhat they all felt it reflected the nineteenth century period and interestingly all three 'felt' the letter 'W' was connected in some way.

Mr Dickinson lost no time in seeing if he could find any leads. He eventually came up with the exciting possibility that the apparition could be that of poet William Wordsworth. Wordsworth was a regular visitor to the area, often staying at Coleorton Hall as a guest of the Beaumont family. He had indeed visited the ruin and in 1811 wrote a poem about the priory; he died in 1850.

My own involvement with the case spanned around nine years involving a large number of visits at varying times of day, the majority being in the evening and into the early hours. The layout of the site presents a few problems for the investigator to conduct covert observation. It is rare to see anyone on the roadside and it is mainly a verge, a bus stop and a field. To stand on the roadside with cameras will inevitably attract unwanted attention. The bus shelter itself is well positioned to offer a reasonable view of the site and is of course beneficial if the weather is bad. I have spent many an hour on a folding chair waiting for cars to come down Belton Lane and illuminate the pitch black ruin before me. Of course the very presence of a human agency may hamper a discarnate entity to form so ideally the bus shelter was best avoided wherever possible.

To observe the road it was best to enter the field and simply watch from an elevated position. For me personally the old railway embankment is the best position as it offers a panoramic view of the entire scene.

These periods of observation were not only to see if an apparition appeared but to watch passing vehicles. One could classify a large percentage of the happenings here as a road ghost scenario. I would observe vehicles to see if there was any sort cf sudden braking, swerving or stopping; if the opportunity presented itself, I could intercept the driver to see what had caused the reaction. This never occurred during my time there, despite a few examples of erratic driving which I judged to be consequence of speeding and, in one case, drunkenness.

The embankment itself is now a path that leads into the village through Grace Dieu woods. Parts of it are quite steep and there is a rather splendid little viaduct over the brook. It was on this embankment that a visitor observed a person wearing cream robes coming through the field. The woman was mystified watching the figure approach the embankment then totally astonished as it walked straight through the timber and wire fence then move soundlessly through the high nettles before going into the embankment itself. By now it had registered that she had seen a ghost. A few seconds later the figure emerged the other side and moved towards the grounds of the school.

Nothing of this nature happened during my many visits and nights here. There were a few frights but attributed to innocent owls, car headlights reflecting, and screaming vixens. I found no atmosphere to the place which is unusual. In a nearby field there is a standing stone. Experiments with a compass to test any electromagnetic fields proved fruitless. The site stands on a tectonic fault line. Such areas are known to harbour unusual electromagnetic properties. There is an interesting theory that suggests such atmospherics can in some way fuel effects such as apparitions. There is also the idea that certain individuals exposed to high concentrations of electromagnetism can experience uneasiness and hallucinatory effects.

I was once asked why a twelfth century nun would be standing at a bus stop – a good question! The only theory I could offer was that what was now the road and bus stop may at one time have been significant to the person in life. The reports of the ghost having no feet may suggest it standing or traversing a lower level of ground as if standing in or 'wading' through the tarmac.

In Andrew Green's *Phantom Ladies*, the ghost is described as old and bent, carrying a shopping bag and is seen shuffling along the road some fifty feet from the bus stop. She is white from head to toe and has a conical hat. There is an idea that the ghost is an old lady who was hit by a car and haunts the roadside, but she is assumed to be a nun because of the priory. An interesting thought but there are no records of a road tragedy anywhere near the site. The shopping bag may well have been a handbag of net a lady of the thirteenth century would carry.

Whatever the explanation, the ghostly nun and of course the six identical white forms have been seen up until 1990 with a flurry of unrest in 1997. The site has secured a reputation as a very haunted place and with good reason.

Belgrave Hall and other museums

Belgrave Hall languishes in the serene little avenue, Church Street in Old Belgrave, Leicester. It has been a period museum since 1936. It was built in 1709 for Edmund and Anne Cradock. Unfortunately Mr Cradock enjoyed it for only a short period, passing away a few months after taking occupancy

Such a grand house would be subsequently inhabited by wealthy wool merchants, hosiery business owners and those requiring a palatial home near the city. John Ellis took the house in 1847. On viewing the hall, Eliza, one of his daughters commented on the place having a ghostly quality to it. John Ellis earned his fortune from many business ventures but his main passion was the railway. The Ellis family remained here until 1928 then hosiers, the Morleys, bought the house.

It is a remarkably quiet little area and easy to walk onto Church Street and step back in time. It is not difficult to imagine how it would have been in times long past. As far as I can ascertain there has been rumoured to be a haunting here since the late 1960s. It is not frightening in any way and sightings are rare indeed. In tends to be confined mainly to the upper rooms and landing where dainty footsteps will be heard on the creaking floorboards.

Over the years the various museum assistants have noticed the tantalising aroma of baking bread wafting through the building, sometimes broth and cooking fruit has also been remarked upon, although no explanation has ever been found.

These unusual happenings may desist for years then occur spasmodically. On rare occasions there are areas that feel very cold and in one instance two assistants entered a cold spot so intense that their own breath hung visibly in the frozen air.

Former museum assistant Tom Smith had only one experience but that drastically reduced his scepticism. Early morning on a winter's day in 1983 Tom arrived and put the kettle on. As usual then he went to pull the window shutters back before lighting the coal fire. He left the kitchen and followed the small corridor as he had done many times before. On his return he walked into an intense force field, the air was charged with static electricity. Tom stopped in his tracks; there was undoubtedly a powerful presence in close proximity. Then, the atmosphere just lifted, nothing to be seen or heard.

In the early part of 1998 there were two sightings reported. Museum assistant Jeannie Bilton was walking up the stairs when she caught a momentary vision of change on the first floor landing, not only was the set-up different but a pair of legs were glimpsed behind a tallboy. Then everything was its normal self again. A few weeks later Mike, the gardener, was in the entrance hall chatting to two of the assistants when out of the corner of his eye he saw someone descend the stairs. As he looked the figure simply vanished. His colleagues noticed his astonishment and asked if he had seen a ghost! Mike did get a good description though, a lady of advancing years wearing a light brown dress. The ghost later became dubbed 'The Terracotta Lady'.

When I first heard of the haunting in the early 1980s, the ghost was called, 'The Green Lady' so presumably someone interpreted it as green or there are two ghosts at Belgrave Hall. The popular belief is that the Terracotta Lady is one of the Ellis sisters, Charlotte, a formidable figure very active in the suffragette movement.

After the Christmas closure in 1998, a museum assistant perused some of the security tapes and discovered an odd effect from the camera facing the formal garden. A fox had activated the infrared lamp that illuminated the area, then a white shape appeared with a misty cloud moving along some feet off the ground. This occurred at nearly 5 a.m. on 23 December.

I had corresponded with the curator, Stuart Warburton, in early December regarding haunting phenomena at the nearby Museum of Technology. In mid-January Mr Warburton telephoned me at my university number.There was something very interesting, could I come over that afternoon?

There are a few individuals claiming to be the first investigator on the Belgrave Hall case. I am pleased to set the record straight: it was Barrie Ratcliffe. After the telephone call I had tried contacting colleagues to attend additionally or on my behalf as it was short notice. Barrie could be there by 4 p.m..

I arrived shortly after with Elaine Greenwood and Susan McLean. Mr Warburton soon arrived and showed us the short segment of footage.

Our verdict was that it was interesting but we could not state it to be a ghost.

A week later a still photograph from the footage was featured in the *Leicester Mercury*. As a result much media interest followed. This led to much interest from various paranormal study groups wishing to get in on the action. There followed the quickest evaluation of a case I have ever conducted. A night was spent in the hall with nothing unusual happening. By mid-February we dispensed with the case so others could examine it.

Various newspapers called Leicester 'The Ghost Capital of the World', I refused to give any verdict to the media, I had no idea what the image was and had no intention of playing guessing games. Renowned experts Maurice Grosse and Dr Alan Gauld were consulted and they kindly offered that the image could be anything from a moth to a banking owl. It will never be satisfactorily resolved.

I did return to Belgrave Hall on three occasions that year, to film a segment for a Japanese television documentary, to meet the International Society for Paranormal Research and to contribute to a four-hour live BBC radio broadcast with representatives of the Association for the Scientific Study of Anomalous Phenomena. I left the case well alone until autumn of 2003 when I returned to spend a night in the hall – with twenty women no less!

The party of ladies were sponsored to spend twelve hours in the hall in aid of charity. I offered my services as 'technical assistant'. On a cold and grim October night I arrived and left my kitbag with museum assistant Norman Baum who had given his time and would host the event. I then went over to the pub to meet the group. I had already met Lynda at her home near Melton; she introduced me to the others before we all adjourned to the Hall.

I set up an internal communication unit from the top floor landing to the base area near the entrance hall. I put an infrared lamp on the first floor landing and placed several thermometers around the building. I then gave a short address to the party on general ghost rudiments before going to the kitchen where I would base myself unless required. I confess to 'defecting' to the pub during a couple of the early watch periods, Norman aided and abetted by sneaking me in and out through the back way!

The girls were very organised and a feeling of cheerful anticipation was in the air that I found would generate a serene atmosphere more likely to be conducive to psychic phenomena; by comparison the night spent in February 1999 had been quite sterile and 'by the book', whereas this was much more relaxed.

An interesting development took place shortly after midnight. Everyone was having a rest break around the blazing fire in the reception hall. I was on the first landing of the stairs looking out over the rear gardens. Several clicks came from the internal communication unit placed nearby. For this to happen someone must tamper with the unit on the top floor, but there was no one up there. Everyone listened intently. I admit to noticing a slight change in the atmosphere and felt my hairs begin to rise. Then, clearly audible, was a rustling of some kind of rich fabric, like satin. I felt it to be emanating from the next floor landing. The girls sat in stony silence looking at each other. When it ceased I very carefully and quietly ascended the stairs. There was no one anywhere although one of the dummies gave me a jolt in the near pitch blackness!

With renewed vigour, the girls began another series of watch periods. At around 4 a.m. the usual tiredness set in. All the girls decided to rest around the fire. I jokingly told them I would go up to the top floor as the ghost would avoid me and come down to them.

One large bed did appear inviting so I thought a quick lie down was in order. I did sense I was being observed so politely explained that I felt tired and was it alright for me to rest my bones. The feeling lifted and I had a pleasant half-hour's rest.

Lynda got a fleeting impression of a man near the pantry; he was in shadow but had a top hat. Several 'orbs' (little opaque dots) were filmed on infrared video camera; there were no temperature drops noted or fluctuations in local electrostatic fields.

Just as dawn approached I asked Dawn to accompany me with a video camera throughout the building as I would try some evocation. We began on the top floor, every room, 'Anyone here?' and stuff like that. No response whatsoever. We then did the next floor with the same results. Just as we were about to descend the stairs I said,' Right, we're off now, goodnight', and just as Dawn switched the camera off we both heard a clear 'Goodnight' in a child's voice! Without doubt it came from the top floor. Dawn and I laughed as we went downstairs; it never happens when you are filming.

The haunted library at Leicester's Guildhall.

The last reported sighting of anything was in 2004 when a young lady saw a grey, undulating mist drift across the garden.

* * * *

The Guildhall Museum in Leicester claims to be 'Leicester's most haunted building'. It certainly has history. It was built in 1390, has served as a town hall, a police station, courthouse and venue for all sorts of civic functions.

It has a phantom black cat that minces around near the little timber staircase in the Great Hall, a cavalier type figure, a large bearded wretch in one of the cells, a dainty lady who inhabits the library, a Victorian 'Bobby' and a large black hound said to appear in the courtyard.

Museum assistant Tony Webster has not seen anything but has heard unexplained footsteps in the Great Hall and a slamming door while in the courtyard. He did note that a large bible in the library was mysteriously tampered with overnight.

Tony Webster points to where odd noises were heard in Leicester's Guildhall.

On the whole the phantoms are a gentle bunch although the cat has nearly tripped people up on the stairs, as they do. I did a talk in October 2005 and was asked if ghosts can harm you. I explained that as the majority of them are merely a product of retained memory and not physical objects, so no, they cannot. A few days later it was reported that a new museum assistant sustained a bad black eye after being 'attacked' by an unseen force. Apparently she was violently flung against a wall on a staircase one evening. This indicates some kind of interactive entity which is quite rare indeed.

You should visit this fine old place, you might be lucky enough to glimpse or sense one of the phantoms but be careful on the stairs, if the cat does not get you, something else might!

* * * *

Another mysterious figure lingers in the Newarke Houses Museum in Leicester. A dark, clerical-looking fellow, he has a long coat or cloak. I was told he is sometimes seen outside the black door near Castle View in early morning. An American tourist actually photographed it by accident whilst taking some photographs of the building!

He is sometimes glimpsed at the top of the oak staircase and mainly occupies the older areas of the building. He once demonstrated his

*Hinckley Museum.
Apparently a ghostly child
inhabits the upper rooms.*

displeasure by causing a display rack of postcards to spin at such speed the contents flew all over the entrance lobby.

* * * *

The Hinckley and District Museum was formed from three cottages that were built in the late seventeenth century. The largest of the three now serves as the main gallery with the other two as smaller annexes.

Originally the cottages may have been occupied by farmers then, when the open fields were enclosed, they moved away and framework knitters then moved in. One of the smaller cottages, number 32, housed a large family of framework knitters in the mid-1800s, the Harrisons. Thomas and Lydia lived here with seven children – a little cramped with just two rooms and an attic!

The cottages were under threat in 1919 when hosiery firm, Atkins, wished to extend their premises. The initial plan was to demolish them to make space for a new factory but Colonel Clive Atkins decided instead to restore them and use them for company business.

As recently as 1991 a group formed a museum trust and in 1995 Atkins leased them the building which opened as a museum a year later.

The Great Hall,
Donington le Heath
Manor House.

Just who is the child who haunts the place? The small boy, obviously distressed as he cries all the time, is dressed in a soldier's uniform. He causes little trouble and the volunteer staff are quite fond of him. He remains a mystery though.

* * * *

Just on the western tip of Coalville is a typical little lane with a few Victorian terraced houses, a short distance along is Donington le Heath Manor House. This is one of the oldest houses in England although the remarkable preservation work creates the idea that it has just been built!

It is believed Robert de Herle bought the land then had the house built between 1288 and 1295. For nearly seven hundred years the house remained a family dwelling. In the early part of the sixteenth century the house was modernised, large rectangular mullioned windows were put in, a new roof was added, a new staircase and alteration of storerooms to create a larger kitchen and parlour.

Sir Everard Digby.

Around this period the house may have been owned by the Digby family. Sir Everard Digby achieved notoriety as one of the conspirators in the Gunpowder Plot; he was a close friend of Guy Fawkes.

In 1670 the Manor House and land was acquired by Thomas Hardy of Osgathorpe. He bequeathed the house to a charitable trust which, until the late 1950s, rented out the house as a tenant farm. The rents were put into the charity and as the tenants could not afford to make any significant changes to the house, apart from essential maintenance, the manor house remained largely unchanged for nearly three hundred years.

In fact the manor house did deteriorate somewhat and after the last tenant departed a farmer bought the pile. The place became derelict and was used to store farm equipment then a number of pigs were housed in it. A rather less than salubrious state of affairs!

In 1963 the house was recognised as an ancient monument and purchased by Leicestershire County Council in 1965 in order to restore the building. This mammoth task was undertaken and took seven years to complete. On 1 July 1973, Donington le Heath Manor House was opened to the public as a museum.

The path where mysterious footsteps have been heard. Donington le Heath Manor House.

Like many such places, the visitor will soon be soaking up the atmosphere, letting their mind wander back trying to imagine past scenarios. Here it is easy to do so. Due to the house being set well away from the road it is eerily quiet. If one was to visit early and be alone and be in that state of mind that harmonises with the atmosphere, one may pick up on a more concentrated atmospheric effect, a presence. A mild feeling of someone, although unseen, moving around or standing observing. Perhaps the presence is pleased or perplexed by one's conduct. If it was the latter perhaps the air temperature would plummet and a sensation of menace would cause one's hairs to lift at the back of the neck.

There are ghosts at Donington le Heath Manor House, sightings are rare but they are heard and sensed.

A housemaid has been seen flitting about. Another of the phantoms, a tall man of seventeenth century appearance with a tall brimmed hat, is thought to be the shade of Sir Everard Digby. Indeed he was a wilful man and of the nature that many ghosts are, stubborn and formidable characters. It is speculated that Sir Everard was enrolled into the Gunpowder Plot by Robert Catesby, an acclaimed horseman and devout Catholic.

In August 1605 Digby's abilities, devotion and extreme wealth would have been welcomed by the conspirators. Sir Everard pledged £1,500 to the conspiracy funds, a massive amount of money. He would take charge of the Plot's midlands operations. He made plans to enlist a large group of disaffected Catholic gentry at Dunsmoor Heath under the pretence of a hunt, they would be told of their involvement once the gunpowder had been fired. Before the news broke the group would capture Princess Elizabeth, who was staying at Coombe Abbey in Warwickshire, and then lead a general uprising.

On Monday 4 November, Digby awaited with a hundred others at the Red Lion at Dunchurch. On the evening of the next day several of the conspirators arrived and imparted that the plot had been discovered. They must make their way to Wales, not a second could be spared. They made a detour to break into the stables at Warwick Castle then onto Norbrook to collect a cache of arms that were hidden there. Near Dudley they were seen by a scout for a posse. They tried to hide in a large wood but were found and easily overpowered. Digby was incarcerated in the Tower of London. As he had played a minor role he was treated leniently unlike many others who were subjected to terrible torture.

Sir Everard Digby was tried separately as he was the only one to plead guilty. His reason for being involved was his religious convictions, his concerns that harsher persecution to Catholics was being planned, and because of the King's broken promises to tolerate Catholicism. He asked in consideration of his status that he be beheaded, this request was refused.

Digby and three others were the first to be executed. This event took place on the dawn of 30 January 1606 in St Paul's churchyard, London. Digby was hung for only a short time and was still alive when he was dragged to the quartering block. There is a legend that when the executioner ripped out his heart and held it aloft declaring, 'Here is the heart of a traitor', Digby croaked defiantly, 'Thou liest'.

I have found little in history of him being at the Donington le Heath house but he must have visited so it is a possibility that Sir Everard haunts the place.

A regular phenomenon is the sound of someone unseen stomping along the south-west gravel path. Mick the gardener was sitting outside when it occurred, the crunching gravel passed him then stopped abruptly at the old stables. Museum Support Officer, Alison Fearn, has heard it more than a few times. She keeps an open mind and is not intimidated by the phantoms.

The museum hosts various events. A recent addition is regular night ghost watches whereby visitors spend the early hours in and around the house in small groups seeing if anything ghostly occurs. During one event a child was recorded crying in 'King Dick's Bedroom' but not heard at the time.

During my visit I found the place quite serene and pleasant, probably the ideal conditions for ghosts.

Braunstone Hall

All of us remember our first day at school. Fear of the unknown for the trembling five-year-old and suppressed tears of the ever-cheerful parent. 'You'll love it here' – these words are of little encouragement as one is led to the fearsome building not knowing if this is forever. Of course, it is not and after the customary tears and the kind and understanding teachers it becomes less harrowing then quite fun.

I would imagine any child being led to Braunstone Hall Junior School after urban decay required the windows to be boarded up would indeed feel terror. The building has been a school from 1933. In its earlier years it appeared quite pleasant – as a palatial house should be. Towards the mid-1980s it became the focus of occasional attacks from vandals and sadly its appearance deteriorated. The first time I saw the place I thought it was closed, all the ground floor windows were boarded up and only a lichen-covered notice indicated it was still a school. The general appearance was bleak and imposing.

The hall was built in 1776 for a wealthy family called the Winstanleys. A huge amount of land would provide hunting, shooting and fishing. They were indeed the lords of the manor. In 1911 modernisation work provided a new wing and an early form of central heating. A large walled kitchen garden would provide not only for the large family but also the large complement of staff.

The surrounding estate was placed under a compulsory purchase order in 1926 and the sprawling Braunstone estate ensued.

Over the years the hall got a reputation for being haunted. This may have originated from a stonemason and labourer being killed during building work. There were tales of a stable hand being accidentally

The nun of Braunstone Hall.

hung, a man throwing himself from a top floor window and a horse-drawn black funeral hearse silently arriving at the hall late at night.

The most enduring phantom is believed to be a nun. May and Georgina Winstanley entered a Roman Catholic convent, the Order of the Sacred Heart, in 1898. Sadly, a year later, May succumbed to tuberculosis. In 1922, Rosemary Winstanley, then aged eight, was walking the corridor from the bathroom to the nursery when she noticed a figure dressed in white moving some feet ahead. Puzzled, Rosemary followed the visitor until it went into the governess's room. She asked the nanny who it was and was told not to worry about it. Several years later, a number of the children contracted measles so it was thought prudent to isolate them in two rooms of the nursery wing. Bessie, the nursery maid, would occupy the governess's room and a bed was set up. One night, terrifying screams disturbed much of the household. Bessie had suddenly awoke to see a young female at the side of her bed. She had a long white dress or robe and her face was obscured by a veil.

In later years Rosemary found out that May Winstanley was a novice nun at the time of her demise and would have had white robes. She also discovered that the governess's room used to belong to May.

Braunstone Hall. A very unsettling place with a dozen ghosts.

The next known sighting occurred in 1973. Alan Jarvis had recently taken the position of caretaker. On a winter's dusk, around 5 p.m. he was sweeping the corridor on the top floor when he noticed a petite figure dressed in white. Alan asked what she was doing when the figure approached him in a fluid manner. He dropped his broom and ran along the corridor then down the stairs in record time. It was quite a while before he dared return that evening but when he did there was no sight of anyone. A few days later he encountered her again, when he felt less intimidated but wary. There were a dozen more sightings and Alan took the sensible attitude that whoever it was had as much right to be here as him.

Alan's daughter, Shirley, was the school secretary for many years and as well as her father's experiences she was well aware of the phantom nun. She had not seen anything herself but would like to. She was instrumental in arranging a night spent in the building in 1988 to help with school funds. The ghost remained aloof on this occasion. A year later she again spent the night there, this time with a party of psychics. The organiser, Brian Johnson, brought a video camera to film the proceedings.

This time many impressions were reported including a large man, possibly a poacher; a lady sitting by a piano; two ladies in rich ball gowns; a 'toff' type character; and a moving misty effect on the top floor. Shirley did not see any ghosts but saw the weird spectacle of invisible hands 'playing' with the hair and dress of her sister, Lynn. Not long after the group left at 4 a.m. Shirley and Lynn retired to the staff room as they would stay until the caretaker arrived. They were almost dozing when they were disturbed by a series of loud bangs echoing through the building. Neither felt compelled to investigate. They felt the psychics had stirred things up a bit.

I spent some time on the case from late 1993 until July 1996, shortly before the school closed. Over this period there were three interesting incidents. After one evening in the school as we were leaving, I realised I had left a cassette recorder in a room on the top floor. The place was in darkness as colleague Dave Holt and I reached the corridor. At around halfway along I felt this intense sensation like an electrical charge, I said to Dave, 'Can you feel that?' The normally highly sceptical Dave replied, 'Yes I can'. We got the recorder and came away, it felt quite intimidating.

After another evening visit we were outside on the forecourt when an excited Shirley ran over. Apparently just as she was leaving she glanced up the staircase and glimpsed a luminous shape. She was over the moon. During a night spent in the school, investigators Ian Harvey and Steve Larter were positioned at the top landing near the main staircase. They were suddenly jolted by a shrill scream and the feeling of something passing behind them at speed. A device for registering electric fields momentarily glowed as if red hot. They were both convinced something of a paranormal nature had occurred.

The building was then left to the elements and ever-increasing vandal attacks. In early 2005 a group of public-spirited residents and former pupils formed 'The Friends of Braunstone Hall'. They would keep an eye on the place and help clean the mess from the outside. While at the County Council offices, founders of the Friends Dorian and Kim Gamble were perusing the school history archives and they found a copy of my booklet *The Ghosts of Braunstone Hall*. Dorian contacted me as he had experienced something unexplained himself. One Sunday morning Dorian was at the front of the hall clearing broken bottles and other debris. He noticed something move swiftly to his left. He looked but there was no one there. It was impossible for anyone to have hidden and it was too large for a low flying bird. He had heard of several recollections and ghostly anecdotes from passers by when working outside the hall. Initially Dorian was sceptical but now less so. Dorian asked if I could help locate historian John Bayldon who had attended one of our nights in the hall in 1994. Dorian's grandfather was part of the American 82nd Airborne Division who were billeted at Braunstone Hall during the Second World War and was very interested in the history of the building. I offered to help and sent on a somewhat poor quality VHS video tape of some of our time at the hall.

Dorian enquired if I wished to return to the hall as he had a set of keys. I would indeed. On a humid Saturday evening in June I met investigators David Paul Booth and Ian Harvey in the Shakespeare pub nearby. We were to meet the full party at 8 p.m. near the tall cedar tree at the rear of the hall. Some of Dorian's group would attend, with Greek investigator Paula Christodoulou and American ghost researcher Linda Tweed arriving later in the evening.

After a relaxing drink, Ian nipped off to a takeaway while David and I casually strolled through the magnificent Braunstone Park. Soon the grim building came into view. After introductions we entered. It was blissfully cooler and nearly all the lower walls and floors were wet. It was a little unsettling to view the damage the building has sustained. However it felt decidedly enigmatic, as it is deceptively large inside with endless rooms. Our base room was the old kitchen block. After a short address to everyone we began the evaluation. Ian returned and set up his camera for a succession of still photographs. David wandered off to take random electrostatic readings while I went for a slow stroll around the hall. Because all the windows were boarded up it was quite dark so I had an image intensifier to help find my way around. As ever the top floor felt a little unnerving, I would return here later on.

Paula and Linda arrived. I gave Paula a video camera and asked her to visit every part of the building. Linda would take random EVP recordings.

David found the old servants' staircase to be worthy of attention and remained there. A Gauss flux monitor was positioned at the top of the stairs (this is where Shirley saw the luminous form) to detect any build up of electromagnetism. It was felt pointless to take temperature readings as the entire building was icy cold!

I sat alone in the darkness in the old governess's room for a while. I then nodded off. I awoke to several profanities. Two of Dorian's group had wandered in totally unaware and I had given them a fright!

We departed at shortly after midnight. No ghosts had shown up. David had photographed a number or 'orbs' on the staircase while Ian was happy with his photography, Paula had taken some useful footage and everyone had a pleasant evening.

A Syston-based group, Ghost UK, spent a night in the hall and reported a number of weird light effects called 'orbs' and a tangible presence. Also several cold spots were detected. A photograph taken outside picked up a strange column of hazy mist.

In July 2005 John Bayldon visited the hall around 10 a.m. on a Friday morning. Several of Dorian's group were present, including his daughter. She was on the small staircase in the west wing when she had a weird experience. A sudden blackness flashed through, she felt a strong electrical current and almost violated. It was as if 'something' had stormed straight through her. She was badly affected by the incident.

The next month Rosemary Winstanley paid a rare visit. Although very frail, she got around and mentioned to Dorian that she would return here in spirit. In the evening a small party of ghost hunters returned. David Paul Booth, Lynda Kinniburgh and I were joined by a few of Dorian's group. It was already dark outside when we began and pitch black in the dank building as I ascended the main staircase alone. On the first floor landing there seemed to be a mild charge in the atmosphere. I could only get up a few stairs then I simply stopped. I do not know what it was but I would not go any further. My scalp tingled for some reason then I simply came away – very strange.

David worked with Lynda, going from room to room with a video camera and digital still camera. Lynda found the place highly charged with psychic remnants.

During a break period I took off into the empty hall with an infrared video camera and a red filtered torch to check out the whole place. I am of the belief that one is more likely to encounter something if alone. On the first floor I peered out through a gap in the shutter and idly gazed over the spinney. A nearly full moon illuminated the huge parkland. It must have been a wonderful sight a century ago, when there were cornfields, the streams and grazing cattle. I then approached the staircase and to my surprise I went up without any trepidation at all. The entire top floor seemed serene but slightly creepy, for want of a better word. I chose a large room with a bit of carpet and lay down in total silence. I awaited the nun.

I nodded off yet again, for around half an hour. I got up and returned downstairs. No nun. Or if there had been, I had missed it.

At around 1 a.m. we finished. Dorian showed us the walled garden and stables before our departure. After a seemingly endless trek around the back paths we arrived. I was dismayed at the walled garden, the pond was still there but the beehives had gone, no doubt the apiary had been attacked by vandals. The stables were silent of screams from the phantom stable hand. We left at just after 2 a.m..

It was most interesting to return to this foreboding place after a nine year period. There seemed to be something missing. Perhaps when it was still a school the children generated the correct conditions for the ghost or ghosts to draw off then manifest later in the day, or in the night.

How to investigate a haunting

An established haunting does not require investigating. However one may update or evaluate an authenticated case. An investigation is to judge if a case is genuine and/or warrants further attention and will originate a case. Some assume that spending a night at a haunt is an investigation but this is merely an additional study. An investigation can last for an hour or several years.

Let us base this example on a contact from a householder who believes a poltergeist outbreak or haunting disturbances have commenced. There have been strange bumps and bangs, doors slamming and something appearing at the foot of the bed in the night.

Firstly I will arrange to visit and interview all witnesses and view areas where alleged incidents have occurred. I may ask many searching questions including queries into any alcohol or drug use, and checking if there might be medication in use that has side effects. Are the doors close fitting or have new doors been fitted? This can cause suction with slamming effects. Sleep paralysis will be explained; this is when someone awakes in the night but is still experiencing dream scenarios and sees someone at the end of the bed. Very often one is paralysed momentarily causing panic. Every mundane scenario has to be explored.

If a loaf of bread has levitated off the table and scattered slices everywhere this is a different matter! I recall a case in 2004 when the family had been driven out. They asked me to come back with them after being away for a day or two. I entered the house first and had a look around, it was fine. The family came into the lounge. We then heard a growl from the kitchen. I went over and said, 'Dog's in here is it?' The response was, 'Ain't got no dog'. I went in and the kitchen was empty!

So a genuine case presents itself. I then explain to the occupants what an investigation may entail, including constant visits (probably all night), cameras everywhere and people trampling all over the place.

As well as cameras and sound recording apparatus there may be other devices applied to create controlled conditions and test for fluctuations in temperature and electromagnetism (ghosts are thought to be composed of photons and neutrons or draw off such particles). Additionally testing of humidity, seismic effects and electrostatic

The author's ghost hunting kit.

discharges may be required. Little 'traps' might be left about to detect pranksters or inquisitive ghosts, such as light coatings of talcum powder on doorknobs (ghosts should not leave fingerprints), fine cotton threads fixed on stairways and passages (to detect if someone passes without breaking them), infrared motion detectors activated by heat sources such as human or animal, and random articles positioned and marked in locked rooms.

While leaving experiments running in key areas there may be need for impartial observers, often throughout the night. The observer will log anything of significance on a notepad or may record an incident with a hand-held video camera.

The occupants will probably want an end to the business. I may offer to locate a cleric to bless the house or a spiritualist medium to calm down and perhaps cease the disturbances. Sometimes nothing works and one is stuck with an invading entity. It may just fade out on its own; these things have no real pattern.

At the end of the investigation one should be able to determine the case's validity and if warranted class it as 'authenticated'.

Some cases are originated by rumour or because a place, such as an ancient ruin, looks 'spooky'. It is merely a matter of going to an old

The author on a ghost hunt in the cellars of the Trip to Jersusalem pub in Nottingham.

ruin or wherever and watching and waiting. Dusk is a good time as our senses alter with the light and dark.

I find exterior locations ideal for casual observation. One may simply turn up and leave at leisure. In theory there should be no electrical supply in an ancient ruin so testing for stray electromagnetic fields is less complicated. I once saw a compass behave very oddly at an outdoor haunt some years ago.

Make allowances for nocturnal creatures, flashing light from distant car headlights and simple optical effects from eyestrain. One should consider dark clothing to blend in with the shadows, a torch, a shooting stick or folding stool, wide brimmed hat or peaked cap as glare from the sky can occur and affect visibility. A good flask and sandwiches are quite essential as well. One might also consider an umbrella! Happy hunting!

Index

Leicestershire Legends

retold by Black Annis

'Let's you and I get a thing or two straight. The name's Black Annis, but you may call me 'Cat Anna' between yourselves – but not to my face, if you value the appearance of yours. There've been days when the aches and pains make me a bit awkward at times, I'll admit as much myself. I've been known to get a bit upset when silly little kids used to play around outside my cave and shout rude remarks like me being an old witch.'

But is she or isn't she? Just an old woman with an attitude problem or actually more of a witch? Herself one of Leicester's best-known legends, Black Annis never quite lets on if she really knows more than she is prepared to say about the Old Ways. But in her direct manner, and with a bit of help from some of her friends, she retells some of the tales of Leicestershire in a way they've never been heard before, with local phrases and dialect rather than written out all posh.

Phantom black hounds, weird goings on where saints were murdered, very odd ways of finding water, pipers who enter underground tunnels and are never seen again, stories about stones, strange lights in the sky, and any number of ghosts – it's all happened in Leicestershire and much more besides, at least if these legends are to be believed.

Black Annis's engaging way of telling of these Leicestershire legends will appeal to all ages and especially to those who think they've heard all this old stuff before.

Specially illustrated by Jenny Clarke, one of Britain's leading tattoo designers.

ISBN 978 1872 883 779. 2004. demy 8vo (215 x 138 mm), 99 + xiv pages, 10 line drawings, paperback. **£6.95**

Also published by Heart of Albion Press

In My Fashion

Starting work in the heyday of Leicester's knitwear factories

Mary Essinger

Winner of the Leicester Writers Club Trude Dub Award for Non-Fiction Book of the Year 2005

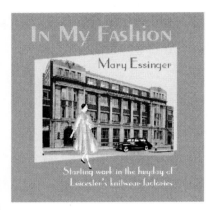

In My Fashion is 'an evocative and enjoyable account of a bygone era. It's neither nostalgic nor whimsical but affectionately remembers the past as it was. There's a great deal of humour and a rich array of characters.'
Jenny Stephens, BBC Radio Drama Producer

Generations of women toiled in Leicester's hosiery factories. This is the story of one of them, a school leaver who started work cutting cotton vests for the Cherub factory in 1949, then went on to work in a dress factory and progressed to the design office.

Highlights in her life at this time included Saturday nights at the Palais wearing Max Factor makeup, weekends hiking to youth hostels, and listening to talk about sex. They are all described with matter of fact humour and innocence.

But this story is not just about one person's factory life – it's about everyone who gets a job, grows up and tries to figure everything out.

ISBN 978 1872 883 793. 2005. 210 x 210 mm, 79 + viii pages, 22 b&w photos and drawings, paperback. **£7.95**

Good Gargoyle Guide
Medieval Carvings of Leicestershire and Rutland
Bob Trubshaw

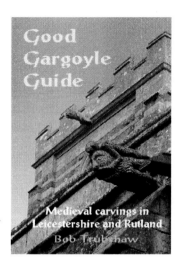

Grimacing gargoyles adorn many of the churches in Leicestershire and Rutland. Alongside them are a wide range of imaginary beasties, foliate faces and Green Men, face-pulling heads, contortionists, and other imaginative figurative carvings. While those on the outside of the churches may be badly weathered, their counterparts inside are usually near-perfect examples of the medieval mason's skills.

Leicestershire and Rutland is fortunate in having more such carvings than in adjoining counties, although this wealth of medieval art has been unjustly overlooked by church historians. These depictions provide a unique insight into the often rather disturbing thinking of the craftsmen who carved them many hundreds of years ago, people who are otherwise almost entirely invisible from historical records.

The aim of the *Good Gargoyle Guide* is to encourage people who would not normally take an interest in church architecture to get out and about hunting further examples of these extraordinary sculptures.

> 'This excellent guide... is a typical Heart of Albion publication: thoroughly researched, nicely presented and also affordable!' John Hinks *Leicestershire Historian*

ISBN 978 1872 883 700. 2004. demy 8vo (215 x 138 mm), 100 + xii pages, 151 b&w photographs, paperback. **£6.95**

Understanding Leicestershire and Rutland Place-Names

Jill Bourne

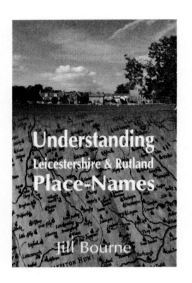

We take for granted the names we use for places. Yet these names are a valuable part of our cultural heritage, providing a detailed insight into the early history of the region. Place-names reveal the otherwise lost voices of our forebears who settled here.

Understanding Leicestershire and Rutland Place-Names analyses the whole range of place-names which occur in Leicestershire and Rutland, most of which were coined between 1,000 and 1,500 years ago. These place-names describe, often in fine detail, the landscape, geology, rivers, buildings, flora, fauna, boundaries, meeting places, roads and track-ways. This book also looks at the distribution of the names, the languages from which they are derived, the successive waves of conquerors and migrants who fought and settled here, and the society they created.

Jill Bourne is an historian, archaeologist and museum professional who has specialised in the area of place-name studies and landscape history for over 20 years.

ISBN 1872883 71 0. 2003, perfect bound. Demi 8vo (215 x 138 mm), 145 + viii pages, 5 maps. **£6.95**

Interactive Little-known Leicestershire and Rutland

Text and photographs by Bob Trubshaw

For seventeen years the author has been researching the 'little- known' aspects of Leicestershire and Rutland. Topics include holy wells, standing stones and mark stones, medieval crosses, and a wide variety of Romanesque and medieval figurative carvings - and a healthy quota of 'miscellaneous' sites.

Some of this information appeared in early Heart of Albion publications (mostly long out of print), but this CD-ROM contains extensive further research. The information covers 241 parishes and includes no less than 550 'large format' colour photographs (all previously unpublished).

There are introductory essays, a glossary and plenty of hypertext indexes.

Runs on PCs and Macs.

ISBN 1 872883 53 2. **£14.95** incl. VAT.

Special offer!

Mail order customers save 17.5% (because Heart of Albion is not VAT registered) = **£12.70**

A Virtual Walk Around Leicester

Max Matthews

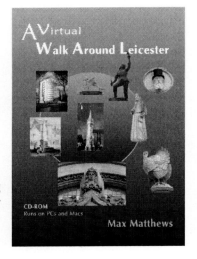

A massive collection of interesting historical information about the city centre.

Contents include:

- Over 1,800 images.

- Detailed histories of all city centre streets.

- Nearly 800 biographies of notable citizens.

- Full text of 1804 *A Walk Round Leicester*

Runs on Windows, Mac and Linux OS. All very computer and user friendly!

ISBN 978 1872 883 748. Published by Heart of Albion 2004. Previously published by Tomax Publications.

Retail price £11.75 (incl. VAT). Mail order customers save 17.5% (because Heart of Albion is not VAT registered) = **£10.00.**

N.B. Because CD-ROMs are much lighter than books, only 80p for post and packing (UK addresses only; overseas add £1.60 p&p).

Explore Folklore

Bob Trubshaw

'A howling success, which plugs a big and obvious gap'

Professor Ronald Hutton

There have been fascinating developments in the study of folklore in the last twenty-or-so years, but few books about British folklore and folk customs reflect these exciting new approaches. As a result there is a huge gap between scholarly approaches to folklore studies and 'popular beliefs' about the character and history of British folklore. *Explore Folklore* is the first book to bridge that gap, and to show how much 'folklore' there is in modern day Britain.

Explore Folklore shows there is much more to folklore than morris dancing and fifty-something folksingers! The rituals of 'what we do on our holidays', funerals, stag nights and 'lingerie parties' are all full of 'unselfconscious' folk customs. Indeed, folklore is something that is integral to all our lives – it is so intrinsic we do not think of it as being 'folklore'.

The implicit ideas underlying folk lore and customs are also explored. There might appear to be little in common between people who touch wood for luck (a 'tradition' invented in the last 200 years) and legends about people who believe they have been abducted and subjected to intimate body examinations by aliens. Yet, in their varying ways, these and other 'folk beliefs' reflect the wide spectrum of belief and disbelief in what is easily dismissed as 'superstition'.

Explore Folklore provides a lively introduction to the study of most genres of British folklore, presenting the more contentious and profound ideas in a readily accessible manner.

ISBN 1 872883 60 5
Perfect bound, demi 8vo (215x138 mm), 200 pages, **£9.95**

Explore Phantom Black Dogs

edited by Bob Trubshaw

Contributors: Jeremy Harte, Simon Sherwood, Alby Stone, Bob Trubshaw and Jennifer Westwood.

The folklore of phantom black dogs is known throughout the British Isles. From the Black Shuck of East Anglia to the Moody Dhoo of the Isle of Man there are tales of huge spectral hounds 'darker than the night sky' with eyes 'glowing red as burning coals'.

The phantom black dog of British and Irish folklore, which often forewarns of death, is part of a world-wide belief that dogs are sensitive to spirits and the approach of death, and keep watch over the dead and dying. North European and Scandinavian myths dating back to the Iron Age depict dogs as corpse eaters and the guardians of the roads to Hell. Medieval folklore includes a variety of 'Devil dogs' and spectral hounds. Above all, the way people have thought about such ghostly creatures has steadily evolved.

This book will appeal to all those interested in folklore, the paranormal and fortean phenomena.

> 'I think this must be the best entry in the Explore series I have seen so far... ' **Aeronwy Dafies** *Monomyth Supplement*

> 'This is an excellent work and is very highly recommended.' **Michael Howard** *The Cauldron*

ISBN 1 872883 78 8. Published 2005. Demy 8vo (215 x 138 mm), 152 + viii pages, 10 b&w half-tones, paperback. **£12.95**

Mystery Big Cats

Merrily Harpur

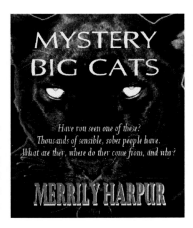

In the past twenty years every county in Britain, from Caithness to Cornwall, has had recurrent sightings of 'big cats' – described as being like pumas or panthers. These anomalous big cats sightings are now running at an estimated 1,200 a year.

Farmers, gamekeepers, ornithologists, policemen and even parents on the school run have all been thrilled – or terrified – to see what they assume is a big cat escaped from a zoo. Yet these big cats are neither escapees from zoos nor, as this book conclusively argues, the descendants of pets released into the countryside by their owners in 1976 when the Dangerous Wild Animals Act made it too expensive to keep big cats.

The questions therefore remain, what are they and where have they come from? With the orthodox explanations overturned, Merrily Harpur searches for clues in the cultures of other times and places. She discovers our mystery felines have been with us for longer than we imagine, and throws unexpected light on the way Western civilisation looks at the world.

Mystery Big Cats is the first serious and comprehensive book on the subject. From the drama of eyewitnesses' verbatim accounts to the excitement of new perspectives and insights into a strange and often terrifying experience – it gets to grips with what is now the commonest encounter with the unknown in Britain.

ISBN 1 872883 92 3. Published March 2006. 245 x 175 mm, illustrated, paperback. **£16.95**

Heart of Albion

Publishing folklore, mythology
and local history since 1989

Further details of all Heart of Albion titles online at
www.hoap.co.uk

To order books or request our current catalogue please contact

Heart of Albion Press
2 Cross Hill Close, Wymeswold
Loughborough, LE12 6UJ

Phone: 01509 880725
email: albion@indigogroup.co.uk
Web site: www.hoap.co.uk